# EVANSVILLE
IN
## WORLD WAR II

# EVANSVILLE

······················· IN ·······················

# WORLD WAR II

JAMES LACHLAN MACLEOD

THE
History
PRESS

Published by The History Press
Charleston, SC
www.historypress.net

Copyright © 2015 by James Lachlan MacLeod
All rights reserved

First published 2015

Manufactured in the United States

ISBN 978.1.62619.675.9

Library of Congress Control Number: 2015948819

*For Jessica, Eilidh, Calum and Gavin.*

# CONTENTS

# ACKNOWLEDGEMENTS

This book was only possible with the help of the people who have already invested countless hours in researching the history of Evansville during World War II and those local archivists who protect our precious historical legacy. I would like to acknowledge the work of Harold B. Morgan, Patrick W. Wathen, Darrel E. Bigham and James and Patricia Kellar, as well as Tom Lonnberg, Pat Sides and Jennifer Greene, all of whom have graciously helped at various stages of this project.

I also acknowledge the Evansville Vanderburgh Public Library; the Evansville Museum of Arts, History and Science; the University of Evansville; the Willard Library; and the University of Southern Indiana, whose physical and digitized collections of local newspapers, artifacts, photographs and cartoons from this period made this research practical.

I would also like to thank my colleagues in the History Department of the University of Evansville and Dr. Ray Lutgring, dean of Arts and Sciences, for their advice, support and encouragement. An Arts, Research and Teaching Grant from the University of Evansville supported some of my research, and Drew Robards was an excellent research assistant.

I want to take this opportunity to pay tribute to two men who took part in World War II: Donald Shaw, my wife's grandfather, who as a young man fought with the U.S. Army in France and Germany, winning both the Bronze Star and a Purple Heart; and my father, Lachlan MacLeod, who as a member of the British Merchant Navy repeatedly sailed the ferociously dangerous waters of the North Atlantic to transport the men and materials on which the Allies depended. To them, and millions like them, we owe our freedom.

Most of all, I want to thank my own children, who put up with a lot of conversations about World War II over the past eighteen months as this book took shape, and Jessica, who not only put up with it but read it and helped to improve it. To the four of you, with my deepest love, this book is dedicated.

James Lachlan MacLeod
Evansville, Indiana
July 2015

# INTRODUCTION

On November 11, 1928, the city of Evansville's first-ever municipal statue was dedicated in a dramatic location at Sunset Park on the Ohio River. The statue was *The Spirit of the American Doughboy* and was the city's memorial to the First World War. In his dedication address, the president of Evansville College, Earl Harper, said, "You must do away with this madman, which is the institution called war,"[1] and he expressed the fervent hope that "not in 100 years shall the heroism of youth again be called upon the battlefield."[2]

These were stirring words, but within less than a decade, the opening exchanges of a second global conflict were beginning to play out half a world away in Asia. Within eleven years, the "madman...called war" would be unleashed again, with almost unthinkable results. Within thirteen years, the United States would be at war once again, in a conflict that would ultimately cost some 405,000 American lives.[3] And within thirteen years, the city of Evansville would once again be called on to send its sons to fight and die in faraway places and to make countless vital contributions to the war effort, most notably in manufacturing. In the process, the city would be transformed.

While traditionally the histories of wars have focused on strategy, tactics and battles, the reality of modern warfare in the middle of the twentieth century was that the single most important element was not any of these things but rather materials; the Pulitzer Prize–winning historian David M. Kennedy has spoken of "the inexorable economic logic of modern warfare, when machines, and the speed and volume of their manufacture, mattered at least as much as men, and the swiftness and precision of their maneuver, in determining the battle's outcome."[4] If what Kennedy says is true, then Evansville certainly played a vital role in helping to ensure that this war—the war over the production of materials—was won by the Allies. And by winning this war, the Allies ensured their eventual victory in the wider war.

What Evansville did during World War II was stunning. Before December 1941, Evansville was a relatively sleepy Ohio River city, badly affected by the Great Depression and with only a couple companies working on military contracts. Bootz Manufacturing was producing a few practice bombs, and Holsclaw Brothers, "Evansville's original war plant," had been producing military tools and dies since the late 1930s.[5] The economic situation was exacerbated throughout 1941 as U.S. industry switched to a war footing and civilian production dropped. The city faced a jobs crisis as employment declined in all its major plants, including Servel, Sunbeam, Briggs, Hercules and Chrysler.[6] And yet, almost incredibly, the city was transformed within a few months into a uniquely productive center of manufacturing for the war effort. Tens of thousands of new workers flooded into Evansville, and two massive new manufacturing centers quickly emerged in the form of the Evansville Shipyard (announced February 14, 1942) and Republic Aviation (announced March 22, 1942).

The shipyard was to make navy vessels called landing ship tanks and by the end of the war had launched 167 of these unglamorous but absolutely essential transport ships. The LST was designed to sail right up onto a beach and then open its huge bow doors to disembark its cargo of tanks and other vehicles directly onto the beach. They were, according to British naval historian Nick Hewitt, "probably the single most important type of ship used in assault landings anywhere in the Second World War…[and were a] massively important piece of technology."[7] No less an authority than British prime minister Winston Churchill remarked that "the destinies of two great empires…seem to be tied up in some God-damned things called LST's,"[8] and on another occasion he said that "the letters 'L.S.T.' are burnt in upon the minds of all who dealt with military affairs in the period."[9]

And Republic Aviation was to manufacture 6,670 of one of the war's most important aircraft, the P-47 Thunderbolt.[10] The Thunderbolt played a vital role as an escort fighter and as a fighter-bomber and, like the LST, was to be of enormous importance in both Europe and the Pacific. The P-47 was one of the most rugged, versatile and effective military aircraft of World War II. One writer said, "By the end of the war all Allied squadrons

Overview of the shipyard with ships on the building ways (right), the launching ways (center) and the outfitting piers (left), May 1942. *Evansville Museum/Evansville Vanderburgh Public Library (EVPL).*

equipped with the P-47 could congratulate themselves on a job well done. In all theatres the crippling losses in personnel and material inflicted on the Axis by Thunderbolt attack had reached staggering proportions."[11] Another commentator on the P-47 said, "There is little question that the Thunderbolt distinguished itself as a potent tactical air weapon in western Europe, that it was reliable and easy to fly. It was also tenacious, and the P-47's highest praise has always come from the men who flew her. She brought them back."[12] No other city in the United States produced both LSTs and P-47s, and had Evansville done nothing else, that alone would have made its contribution to the war effort unique.

But there was, of course, much more to Evansville's unique contribution than transport ships and fighter airplanes. As Darrel Bigham has observed, "As significant as the Evansville Shipyard and Republic were, most war workers were employed in factories that had existed before early 1942. Vanderburgh county firms would, by March 1944, receive nearly $600 million in defense contracts...[and] forty-eight Evansville businesses did some sort of war work."[13] Of all these businesses, it is possible that none was more important than the Chrysler plant, which, in "one of the miracles of American Production,"[14] was in less than five months transformed from a factory producing 275 Plymouth automobiles per day into the Evansville Ordnance Plant. This plant produced the mind-boggling number of 3,264,281,914 rounds of .45-caliber ammunition, which amounted to 96 percent of all the .45 ammunition manufactured in the United States during World War II.[15] In addition, the Servel Corporation manufactured wing panels for the Republic Thunderbolts; Sunbeam Electric did vital work to shift .45-caliber shell casings from brass to steel; Hoosier Cardinal produced plastic domes for such iconic U.S. bombers as the P-29; International Steel made bridges, piers and pontoons; Briggs Indiana manufactured wings for navy airplanes; and the Faultless Caster company produced millions of fuses and millions of navy tracer rounds.[16] Many other plants large and small switched over from what they had been doing before and manufactured a huge array of products for the war effort, leading one industrialist to refer to the Evansville war plant workers as "the army left at home."[17]

It was indeed an army. Thousands of Americans flooded into Evansville from all over the country, and the city's manufacturing workforce more than tripled from eighteen thousand to sixty thousand, with many of these jobs being well paid. It was a stark contrast with the Depression years, when Evansville had seen 25 percent unemployment.[18] Migration on this scale also put enormous strains on the existing housing stock, and it was clear from the very start that extraordinary steps would have to be taken to provide living accommodations for all the new workers and their families. It was assumed that the city might have to deal with up to forty thousand new arrivals by the end of 1942. Building projects began immediately, and by the end of the war, Evansville had constructed no less than six large federal housing projects, one of which was for African Americans, as well as at least seven other developments, privately built with federal financial help.[19]

Activities like this were happening all over the United States, and this, perhaps, is what makes Evansville such an interesting case study. The story of Evansville in World War II is not just the story of a unique contribution to the war effort, but it is also in many ways a fascinating reflection of the wider American experience during the war. In Evansville, as in the rest of the United States, World War II brought an end to the Great Depression and signaled the beginning of a new era of expansion and success. With astonishing speed, companies and corporations switched over from domestic production to war production, and millions of people moved around the country. David Kennedy has observed that "fifteen

As the shipyard was being constructed, one gantry crane would be used to build the next, August 1942. *Evansville Museum/EVPL.*

million persons—one out of every eight civilians—changed their county of residence in the three and a half years after Pearl Harbor."[20] And so Evansville was clearly part of a highly significant and unprecedented movement of the American population. Women moved into the workforce in every part of the country, and the challenges and opportunities that are seen in Evansville reflect this wider phenomenon. The same might be said of the tensions surrounding race relations, as African Americans not only moved into parts of the country where they had not lived in large numbers but also moved into sectors of the workforce that had previously excluded them. Evansville's struggles with the issue of prostitution in this period were also very much a reflection of what happened across the country. The military had to deal with the recreational activities of millions of servicemen in thousands of locations, and it was a monumental task.

Further, Evansville's experience of being asked to produce a staggeringly wide array of different items for the war effort also mirrored the experience across the country, as the demands of a complex modern war effort required an astonishing number of parts. It must be remembered that the United States was not just supplying its own military forces but also in significant ways those of its allies: by 1944 the United States was supplying 10 percent of the Soviet Union's military materials and 25 percent of Great Britain's.[21] Indeed, the very first LST built by the Evansville Shipyard—LST 157, launched in October 1942—ended up as part of the British Royal Navy and participated in the British campaigns in Asia.

Another important way in which Evansville's experience reflects wider national trends is in the organization of war material production. The American production effort was neither an action of the federal government nor of private enterprise but was instead a complex and highly flexible mix of the two. The Evansville Shipyard, for example, was operated under the auspices of the Department of the Navy and had senior navy personnel overseeing operations, but it was operated by a private company, the Missouri Valley Bridge and Iron Company.[22] The factory building P-47s was subject to the approval of the War Department but was operated by the Republic Aviation Corporation. All of the raw materials, and even some completed parts for the ships and airplanes, were supplied by other local companies as well as some from farther away. It is notable that these two huge enterprises were brought to Evansville in part because of the lobbying done on the city's behalf by local industrial magnates—whose own companies then benefitted greatly from the resultant war-related production. The key player in bringing the Evansville Shipyard to the city was Walter G. Koch, the vice-president of International Steel; his company ended up providing much of the steel for the construction of LSTs in Evansville. And according to the *Sunday Courier and Press* of March 22, 1942, the four figures who helped bring the Republic Aviation plant to Evansville were senior executives in Hoosier Lamp and Stamping, Servel, Hoffman Construction and International Steel, all companies that were to play pivotal—and profitable—roles in the success of the plant.

The final way in which the Evansville experience was a reflection of the American experience was that while the Second World War has recently been called "the most destructive event in recorded human history,"[23] the city itself did not directly experience the physical impact of war. Like the rest of the continental United States (other than a handful of Japanese balloon bombs on the West Coast), Evansville was not under any attack; no bombs fell on the River City. It did, however, experience casualties. When Evansville's contribution to World War II is discussed, it should not be forgotten that 459 local men were killed during the war. It is striking when examining the local newspapers during the war that there was an almost daily litany of reports about local men being killed, wounded, listed missing or taken prisoner. The first Evansville casualty of the war was George James Wilcox, killed beside 2,403 other Americans at Pearl Harbor on December 7, 1941, and news of death in battle was being received in Evansville long after the war was over. The death of Lieutenant John E. Baker, for example, was not confirmed until January 1946. The drawn-out nature of the pain did not end there, of course, as there was a significant and inevitable delay in repatriating the bodies of those who had been killed overseas; Sergeant Harold W. Wolf's remains did not return home until May 1950.

This book will discuss all of these issues, starting with a chapter covering the shipyard and moving on to look at Republic Aviation and some of the other most significant war plants. Chapter 4 will then discuss the most significant social issues, including gender, fundraising and race, but also the often neglected area of prostitution. The provision of housing and its attendant issues will be discussed in Chapter 5, and finally, there will be a chapter that reflects on Evansville's war dead. Before any of that though, an obvious question arises: why did all this industrial activity happen in Evansville? It is with this question that the book will begin.

# 1
# HOW IT CAME TO BE

It is important to emphasize that what happened in Evansville between 1941 and 1945 was not simply a spontaneous product of World War II—the wartime transformation of Evansville did not happen by accident, and millions of dollars of war contracts did not just happen to arrive in Evansville. Indeed, the whole story could have been very different—in September 1941, there were very real fears that the nationwide prioritization of defense projects would have devastating consequences for a city like Evansville, dominated as it was by non-defense industries. Instead, a fascinating and highly effective coalition of business, labor and political leaders worked together in a variety of ways to ensure that, far from becoming a ghost town, Evansville would become a boomtown.

As Patrick W. Wathen has observed, Evansville's prescient civic leaders "knew cities like Evansville could become the first casualties once the country went on a full war footing. Rather than watch opportunities pass, they chose to lead the city into the most vibrant period of its history."[24] As early as March 1941, a group was established called the Manufacturers Association Defense Committee, chaired by Thomas J. Morton Jr., president of the Hoosier Lamp and Stamping Corporation, and dominated by the big local companies. By April, they had conducted "a survey of all available machine and personnel facilities within 50 miles of Evansville to make it possible to pool resources and get more defense work." Lieutenant Colonel William Carter Bliss, the liaison officer between the military's procurement arms and local manufacturers, was extremely impressed.[25] By the summer of 1941, the chamber of commerce had already assembled data detailing Evansville's "resources, transportation and industrial facilities and other advantages," and this had been shared with "practically everyone in Washington from the President down." The results, however, were disheartening, with Arthur P. Eberlin of the chamber reporting, "It looks like Evansville is the forgotten country, or no-man's land…we do not seem to be able to interest any one in Washington in this part of the state…It is unfortunate, but nevertheless true, that notwithstanding the fact that petitions, briefs, brochures and special committees have been resorted to, Evansville is still without a defense plant." The money being spent on defense contracts in Evansville was, he asserted, "only a drop in the bucket compared with money being spent elsewhere."[26]

The worry was palpable. On Tuesday, July 1, 1941, a committee of local leaders assembled at the Lamplight Inn on Second Street to further address the problems that they believed the city would face; it was, according to the *Evansville Press*, "an aggressive effort to bring defense industries to Evansville and to obtain defense contracts for established industries." The meeting was called by the Central Labor Union but also included such men as Democratic mayor William Dress; Louis Ruthenburg, president of Servel; F.B. Culley, president of the chamber of commerce; and C.B. Enlow, president of National City Bank. Within two weeks, Mayor Dress and several other members of the committee traveled to Washington, D.C., where, in what was to be a vital turning point in Evansville's history, they met with senior figures in the federal government's Office of Production Management (OPM).[27] Sidney Hillman, the associate director of the OPM, was struck by the fact that Evansville was the first city in the country to send a delegation that represented not only city government but also labor and management and that it defined the city's "situation as a community problem."[28] As a lifelong union activist, Hillman might well also have been impressed that three of the five members of the Evansville delegation were from the Central Labor Union. In the words of the *Indianapolis Star*, Hillman gave "more than an hour and a half of his time when they went to Washington to present the problem. Big shots usually get only 15 minutes with this chief."[29] As a direct result of this meeting, Hillman suggested that Evansville might be made a test city where an OPM engineer would assess the impact of the prioritization of defense projects. On their return to Evansville, Mayor Dress followed up with a letter to Hillman urging that this suggestion be acted on.[30]

While they waited to see what the OPM would do, the Evansville community was not idle. In September 1941, the committee urged Mayor

Cartoon by Karl Kae Knecht illustrating the dramatic success of the Evansville community working together to bring war contracts to the city, April 1942. *University of Evansville/EVPL.*

Dress to involve other cities in the efforts to protect existing industries from the damage done by defense prioritization, and he duly organized a conference in Chicago, to which six hundred mayors of medium-sized cities were invited. Dress outlined a nightmare scenario where an "unemployment catastrophe" would bring disorder to the country's streets and disruption to the national defense effort: "Let us not forget that starving, jobless men and women can constitute a sixth column of wandering, confused people, which will be more devastating to our defense efforts and to our efforts to supply the fighting democracies of the world than any fifth column that an enemy could drop out of the skies. Patriotism and national unity can not thrive on unemployment."[31]

The conference was duly held in Chicago on September 12. Also in September, the AFL-affiliated United Auto Workers of America circulated a petition to be sent to the OPM, urging that it consider Evansville for defense contracts, claiming that Evansville needed this more than any other city in the state.

On September 8, however, city comptroller Gilbert H. Bosse was informed by a wire from the OPM that it had indeed made Evansville a test city to study the impact of defense priorities on existing civilian production. One day later, Ralph Kaul and August Wilks of the OPM arrived in Evansville and met with many representatives of labor unions, as well as political and business leaders. In words that turned out to be prophetic, Kaul stated that the solution to Evansville's potential unemployment problem was not to be "found in attempting to maintain civil production. The real answer is in converting into defense production." Even more prophetically, the pair met representatives of Sunbeam, Servel, Chrysler, Hoosier Lamp and Briggs,[32] all of which would subsequently play a huge role in Evansville's war effort. Kaul received detailed information about "past, present and prospective employment in 21 major manufacturing establishments," as well as a four-point plan that was submitted by the committee of civic leaders. The plan called for preferential consideration for the city, and its final point requested "acquisition of defense industries."[33] A mere ten days later, the OPM announced that Evansville was to be certified as "an area entitled to preferred consideration in awarding defense contracts because of threatened unemployment caused by curtailment of materials." It meant that contracts could come to Evansville without going through a competitive bidding process, and there is little doubt that this crucial decision by the OPM cleared the path for all that would follow.[34] The head of the OPM's contract distribution division, Floyd B. Odlum, said that Evansville would now get defense contracts, "or there must be some damn good reason why they don't." In a statement that was to signal the transformation of Evansville, he said, "I fully expect the Army, Navy and Maritime Commission to place defense contracts there, even if they are not based on low bidding but merely negotiated in an effort to solve the priorities unemployment problem."[35] The certification itself was sent to William Knudson, director general of the OPM, by Odlum on October 7; he requested that Knudson "cause this certification to be executed" and transmitted to the secretary of war, with a copy to be forwarded to the secretary of the navy.[36] On October 10, the secretary of the navy wrote to Knudson, thanking him for the Evansville data and saying, "I shall go over this myself and will then make it available to Captain Fisher of the Navy Department, who is in charge of the Naval Contracts Distribution Division."[37] Evansville, it seemed, was getting all its ducks in a row.

It is also clear that Congressman John Boehne Jr., himself an Evansville native and a World War I veteran, was working hard behind the scenes on Evansville's behalf. He met and corresponded with William Knudson[38] on one occasion in late December, directly asking for "one of the bomber or bomber assembly plants for Evansville."[39] He did not stop there. He wrote to the president himself, asking that he put pressure on Robert P. Patterson, undersecretary at the War Department, on behalf of Evansville, and it seems to have worked. In January 1942, the *Evansville Press* reported that "President Roosevelt had written Mr. Patterson, on request of Representative Boehne, directing his attention to the need for further war orders at Evansville." On January 9, Boehne had a long meeting with Patterson and emerged with a very positive report: "Large war orders for both Sunbeam and Servel plants are in the making, the undersecretary of war assured me…In fact, he said every available plant in Evansville that can turn out any war product will be used. He was interested in the report that Chrysler officials are working for a contract for their plant in Evansville and told me that there was no doubt that they will get it." Intriguingly, he also said that "new plant facilities for another highly important wartime weapon also are being considered for Evansville [but] further details couldn't be divulged."[40]

The first of these plant facilities was the Evansville Shipyard, announced to a shocked population on February 14, 1942. While it was clearly a product of all the groundwork discussed above, a key role was also played by Walter G. Koch, the vice-president for sales for International Steel. The *Evansville Courier* said that their informed local sources gave all the credit to Koch, saying that he had been working on it for weeks and had spent a lot of recent time in Washington, D.C., working to bring the shipyard to Evansville. The various complexities involved in bringing a navy shipyard to Evansville were fleshed out further in that evening's local newspaper. Walter G. Koch, said the *Evansville Press*, "first heard of the proposal to build an inland shipyard several months ago through contacts with officials of the shipbuilding company. At the time he proposed to these officials that if they were successful in obtaining a contract from the Navy Department that Evansville be given serious consideration as a site. Continuous contact was kept with the officials of the shipbuilding company and a promise was given that Evansville would receive consideration."[41] Koch had then reportedly called a meeting with Mayor Dress and some key leaders of local industry and business to discuss the plan and to secure their support; having got their "whole-hearted support," he called the company and invited them to come inspect the projected riverfront site. A few days later, officials and shipyard engineers came to do the inspection and then went back to talk further with the navy. According to the *Press*, "A brief was prepared outlining Evansville's advantages, among them being transportation facilities, labor supplies, nearness of the site to the heart of the city, management and labor cooperation and the safety of the site in its relationship to flood conditions, [as well as] raw material factors." Koch traveled back and forth to Washington, D.C., several times to discuss the site, and E.H. Barkmann, chief engineer of the Missouri Valley Bridge and Iron Company, came to Evansville to get detailed information. On February 13, 1942, barely two months after Pearl Harbor, Congressman Boehne announced that the Navy Department was going to construct what the *Evansville Courier* of February 14 called "a very large shipyard" to build an unlimited number of three-hundred-foot boats "using all possible facilities we can lay our hands on." The precise nature and purpose of the vessels was not revealed at this time.[42]

The shipyard, then, came to Evansville because of a combination of the groundwork set in place over a period of months by a variety of players and the "closing" skills of Walter G. Koch and a handful of others. Much the same story can be told about the coming of Republic Aviation. The reason that thousands of airplanes ended up being built in Evansville was, once again, that local businessmen used their influence and their contacts, alongside the wide range of lobbying efforts discussed already, to persuade key decision makers that Evansville was the place that they should locate. In this case, the crucial player was C. Nelson Smith, the vice-president of the Hoosier Lamp and Stamping Corporation, who had a personal relationship dating back to 1925 with his "old St. Louis friend and neighbor," airline executive Ralph S. Damon.[43] In 1941, Damon was appointed president of Republic Aviation, based in Farmingdale, New York, and almost immediately used his Evansville contact to establish a subcontracting role first for Hoosier Lamp and later for Servel. According to the *Sunday Courier and Press*:

> *Just before Pearl Harbor, Republic was advised further expansion would have to be at an inland location. At the same time they were told of the greatly multiplied need for the types of planes they were making and pressure was brought to bear on them to quickly arrange for additional production. Nelson*

Walter G. Koch, considered by most to be the architect of the shipyard coming to Evansville, speaking to an assembly of workers at International Steel, October 1942. *Willard Library.*

*Smith realized Evansville had already arranged to make an appreciable part of the airplane structure; that it had additional fabricating capacity; excellent semi-trained labor skilled in sheet-metal manufacture, as well as a position nearly central to the sources of needed materials and adequate shipping facility.*[44]

Smith worked with A.J. Hoffman of Hoffman Construction, Louis Ruthenburg of Servel and Rufus Carnes of International Steel "to assist Republic in such a way that they could only choose Evansville as a location." They agreed to work together and, with the mayor and local government on board as well, arranged to do whatever was necessary to make sure that both Republic and the federal government were satisfied.[45]

And satisfied they certainly were. On Sunday, March 22, 1942, a Republic announcement, approved by the War Department, revealed that the plant was coming to Evansville. In it, Damon commented, "It seemed to me that

Republic Aviation could safely entrust its operations in vital war production to a city which showed such teamwork and also had the natural advantages possessed by Evansville."[46] Ground was broken on a rainy day in April, with Nelson Smith, literally, right in the center of the picture. George Meyer, Republic's general manager for the Evansville facility, praised the area and especially its people. He said that he had at first focused on the logistical assets of Evansville, but

> *good as I discovered these to be, I quickly found the people we had to work with were also among the advantages of Evansville. I have had the greatest possible co-operation from everyone with whom my work has brought me in contact. Here is a region widely known for the ability of its people to produce. That ability comes largely from the character and skill of intelligent manpower—the patriotic manpower that is playing such an important part in the fight against enemies of our country. Our job is production, and I*

A powerful symbol of what could be built in Evansville by the military and industry working together: a V-trestle pier, with the shipyard visible in the left distance, November 1943. *Willard Library.*

*am confident that southern Indiana will give us able hands and stout hearts and that together we will do our part in backing our fighting forces with the finest weapons American ingenuity can devise.*[47]

What is very clear about the story of Evansville in World War II is that a wide range of local men used their networks to put the city on the map. As pressurized federal officials scrambled to turn an under-militarized and largely isolationist country into the world's most formidable superpower on an almost-impossible time schedule, they were, of course, open to suggestions. It is possible that they were desperate for suggestions. So Evansville's labor leaders, with connections to organized labor all over the country, were able to push the city into the national defense conversation. Members of Evansville's business elite, also with countrywide connections and networks, were able to do the same from their position. And lastly, Evansville's politicians were able to take advantage of their own connections—all the way up to and including Franklin Delano Roosevelt—to ensure that the city received fair consideration when defense contracts were being distributed. Despite a history of fairly profound political divisions, and of bitter battles between labor and management,[48] in the crucial months of 1941–42, they were able to find a way to synergize for the greater good of their community, with transformative results for the city. It is to these results that this book now turns, starting with the Evansville Shipyard.

# THE EVANSVILLE SHIPYARD

As has been seen, it did not take long for the war to come to this sleepy city on the Ohio River, and it did not come in a way that even well-informed observers of Evansville might have predicted. On February 14, 1942, the *Evansville Courier* revealed that a shipyard was coming and that it was to be located on some forty-five acres of mostly derelict land along the Ohio River between the Mead Johnson Terminal and the Southern Indiana Gas and Electric Company Power Station. Headquarters for the project were set up at the corner of Second and Sycamore Streets, very close to the yard's proposed site. Congressman Boehne said that "the navy told him to tell the people of Evansville that they were expected to 'deliver the goods' including housing facilities, labor, lumber, etc."[49]

Later in the day, more details were added to the dramatic and transformative story. Some surprisingly specific information emerged about the ships—they were to be "new type ships…approximately 300 feet long, 50 feet wide and of sufficient light draft when empty to permit their being forwarded to the Gulf of Mexico under their own power." The ships were to be made entirely of steel and would have diesel power. The yard would operate under direct navy supervision with Lieutenant Frank G. Healey as the navy officer who would be in charge. Healy was interviewed by telephone by the *Evansville Press* and revealed that while he would remain based in Jeffersonville, Indiana,[50] he planned to visit the Evansville yard often. He said that the Navy Department expected "to be producing the new ships within three months."[51]

Evansville's business and civic leaders were in no doubt as to the significance of the project for the River City. Henry Bohnsack, the president of International Steel, was clear about the implications: "The urgency of this project, the speed with which it will get under way, the number of workmen that will be employed, assures Evansville labor that there is no need of Evansville workmen to go elsewhere for employment." Mayor Dress said in a stirring statement that the impact on the future of the city was not known:

*At once, however, questions of labor supply and housing arise which call on all our resources for immediate solution. As mayor, I want to assure the contractors and Navy Department that Evansville will solve their problems so that national defense can be expedited with no inconvenience to those who have seen fit to put confidence in our ability to do the job. We are entrusted with an industry that is new to us and our civic conduct toward this project will be the measure of our worthiness. In this connection I call upon every*

Construction of the launching ways and the cofferdam is well underway, with downtown Evansville in the distance, June 1942. *Evansville Museum/EVPL.*

*industry in Evansville and all our citizens to lend whatever aid is necessary to prove that in Evansville it can be done.*[52]

And in Evansville it could indeed be done. Within three days, the first drafting table was in place at the historic McCurdy Hotel overlooking the Ohio River, and six engineers were beginning work to design the shipyard.[53] A few days later, a shipyard job office had opened, and the *Evansville Courier* of February 27, 1942, reported "a steady hum of activity" there that saw hundreds of men pick up applications for jobs at the yard. By early March, federal condemnation proceedings for the few existing buildings on the site were filed in Indianapolis and then transferred to federal district court in Evansville to clear titles to the land for the yard. A check for $76,374.35 was deposited to pay for any land claims that arose, and on March 12, the *Evansville Press* reported that "approximately 70 men began preliminary construction operations Thursday on the new naval shipyards along the Ohio River in Evansville…Surveying crews were busy from one end of the yard to the other. At least three crews were staking their surveys on different sections. At the same time, one crew of men was at work stacking newly arrived materials for construction of plant facilities." It was not a simple task, as the site had to be cleared, excavated and then graded before thousands of square yards of reinforced concrete could be poured for what would be the construction area—what in shipyard parlance was called the "building ways." Miles of pipes and wires were pre-installed under the concrete for "underground oxygen, electric, compressed air, acetylene, water, gas and drainage lines"[54]—there were no overhead lines in the entire yard.[55] Scaffolding and cranes were built, as were a variety of offices and storerooms. An enormous cofferdam was built into the Ohio River—a concrete wall that enclosed part of the river, which was then pumped dry to allow the launching ways to be constructed down into the river. And then four docks for outfitting were built, each of which could handle two ships. The final cost of building the shipyard was a staggering $6.4 million.[56]

Seven months later, the *Sunday Courier and Press* of October 25, 1942, reflected on the unlikely accomplishment: "A year ago Evansville's most enthusiastic river men or industrialists would have called this strictly an inland city, and would probably have hooted at the idea of building seagoing ships along our riverbank. In less than a year that selfsame riverbank has been turned from a littered dump dotted with squatters' shacks to an up to date shipyard."

And the shipyard had not just been built; it was already building ships. In fact, in an astonishing feat of engineering and ingenuity, shipbuilding

The first keel is laid at the Evansville Shipyard, with construction of the yard itself clearly going on around it, June 25, 1942. *Evansville Museum/EVPL.*

began long before the yard itself was complete. The first keel for an LST, constructed at International Steel's plant on West Tennessee Street, was laid at the shipyard on June 25, 1942, in a simple but dramatic five-minute ceremony. Commander Phillip Lemler of the U.S. Navy's Bureau of Ships spoke to the audience of several hundred workers, and "while the crane maneuvered the keel, a flag was raised above the yard and whistles shrieked, indicating boat construction was underway, three months after the Missouri Valley Bridge and Iron Company began building the yard itself." Mayor Dress referred to the yard coming to Evansville as a "dream" and said, "If we all help this yard will turn out ships that will help turn the tide of battle." As soon as the brief program ended, workers hurried back to their jobs.[57]

They hurried back to begin turning "the tide of battle" in the Second World War. For the words of Mayor Dress were in many ways to prove prophetic. At exactly this moment, in June 1942, one of the most vital battles of the war—and perhaps of the twentieth century—was reaching a critical tipping point. This was the Battle of the Atlantic: the struggle between the

Mayor Dress speaking at the laying of the first keel, predicting that these ships would "help turn the tide of battle." June 25, 1942. *Evansville Museum/EVPL.*

German navy's U-boats and the escorted Allied merchant ships that were carrying Britain's vital supplies across the ocean. The battle was, among other things, a race to see if more ships could be sunk than could be built to replace them—and in mid-1942, it was not looking good for the British. British prime minister Winston Churchill famously remarked that "the only thing that ever really frightened me during the war was the U-boat peril."[58] In June 1942, Churchill must have been at his most frightened because that was the month that saw Allied losses at their highest, with over 700,000 tons of shipping sunk; between January and July 1942, the Allies lost shipping that amounted to 3 million tons.[59] To reduce this battle to statistics is to do it a disservice—in the words of C.L. Sulzberger, "The Atlantic battle was a dirty, cold, grueling business. Nerves were constantly on edge. Whether in the quivering, claustrophobic submarines, dodging among depth bombs, or aboard the destroyers zigzagging overhead, always on the alert for telltale sonar signals…The Battle of the Atlantic became brutal and merciless."[60]

Brutal and merciless as it was, the tide began to turn in the summer of 1942. After that point, Allied losses declined, German U-boat losses rose and, critically, Allied shipbuilding took off. Most especially, American shipbuilding took off, and eventually, as Gerhard Weinberg has said, "the construction curve continued to rise dramatically even as losses leveled off. Contrary to German expectations, the United States not only built enormous numbers of ships of standardized design more and more quickly; it could man and arm them."[61] Crucial to this process was the rapid construction and activation of shipyards like the one in Evansville. Even though the LSTs played no direct role in the Battle of the Atlantic and not a single Evansville LST was lost in the Atlantic,[62] their construction in Evansville allowed other yards in other parts of the United States to construct the merchant ships to carry war materials and the destroyers, cutters and corvettes to escort them. All of this was done on a huge scale and at a breakneck pace. By 1943, the shipyard in Richmond, California, was building cargo vessels—the famous "Liberty Ships"—in seventeen days.[63] In October 1942, War Production Board chief Donald M. Nelson said, "Hope is being carried to the world in American ships. The responsibility of transforming this hope into reality falls on the shipbuilding industry."[64] As the flag was raised and the whistles shrieked to mark the laying of the first LST keel in Evansville, they were also marking the beginning of the end of the Battle of the Atlantic.

The stakes were high in the middle of 1942, and everyone knew it; nothing could be left to chance. Commander F.M. McWhirter, the navy's district security officer, wrote to the yard's manager to say, "The danger of espionage and sabotage to all facilities producing war material is ever-present. Your shipyard is vital to the success of the whole war effort. It must produce without interruption. A well-planned and maintained security program is the only possible defense against possible devastating enemy action."[65]

Despite taking such steps as examining all incoming and outgoing lunchboxes and sandbagging transformers, further security concerns were soon to threaten access to one of Evansville's iconic locations—Reitz Hill, which dominates the West Side of Evansville and offers a commanding and spectacular view of the downtown and the Ohio River. In late May, a petition to the Board of Works and Safety from the Navy Department and the Missouri Valley Bridge and Iron Company sought the closure of Reitz Hill to all traffic for the rest of the war. The hill looked down on the new shipyard, and the navy's lawyer argued that closing it was essential for "protection against sabotage and espionage." The school board had already given permission [Evansville Reitz High School sits on top of the hill] to close the side of the hill overlooking the shipyard, and there were plans to fence off the hill. It was reported that "the petition pointed out that the police had confiscated pictures of the shipyard taken by an amateur photographer [who]…surrendered the pictures when he discovered the top of the hill was posted with signs warning against taking pictures."[66] The authorities felt that they had to go further and completely close Lemcke Avenue for fear of photographs being taken from a moving vehicle. Reitz Hill was a popular spot for local couples, and the *Evansville Press*'s "Home Front" column clearly thought that the measure was excessive, joking that the navy was "afraid of peekers not petters."[67] Six days later, the board further delayed its decision but indicated that it did not think that closing the street was essential. The street, and Reitz Hill, remained open for the duration of the war, although it was kept under surveillance by shipyard security guards using telescopes.[68]

Reitz Hill may have remained open to amorous locals, but strict security restrictions were later put in place on the river itself with a twenty-four-hour Coast Guard patrol controlling access to a new restricted zone. The *Evansville Courier* of September 1, 1942, reported that the area was almost two miles long and that "no cameras or firearms may be carried on a boat passing through the area. A special operations license is required of all commercial vessels." All vessels had to report their intentions to move, and the Coast Guard would then inspect them; all on board had to have identification cards. It all might seem a little redundant, given Evansville's location, but in a war where the battle over intelligence was central, and when so much of that battle was decided by seemingly innocuous scraps of intelligence, nothing was to be left to chance.[69]

Evansville, then, was undergoing a transformation that was as dramatic as it was rapid, and the speed with which it all took place is one of its most striking aspects. On March 1, 1942, the *Sunday Courier and Press* observed in an editorial called "Our War Job" that "we have done some amazing things in the 12 weeks since Pearl Harbor" and then continued:

> *We have pulled our auto industry up by the roots…Our refrigeration industry* [has] *already shifted to war work…A shipyard which will work thousands at top production speed is being installed on the river banks and many other large contracts either have been signed or will be within a few days. We are now producing large quantities of military supplies. Within a relatively few weeks this production will actually be multiplied by several hundred. Guns, boats, ammunition and planes will be leaving Evansville in a great stream along with a hundred other items so urgently needed that they mean literally the difference between life and death for our men in the Army and Navy. A few months ago Evansville seemed to have been left out of the war industrial program. It now becomes one of the most active spots in the country….Not all of us can wear a uniform or do factory work. But*

*all of us can and must co-operate in providing for those who can. We must quit rejoicing over the business boom which is just around the corner and remember that what we have in prospect is not a picnic but a hard job which may prove extremely disagreeable except for the thought that it's helping to win the war.*

What is remarkable about this editorial is how down to earth it was and how willing it was to acknowledge the complexity of the job at hand. While it was an impressive sign of the city's ability to see the "big picture," at the same time, the city had to wrestle with the minutiae of building oceangoing ships in Evansville at a brand-new location. This was a highly complex business with, literally, many moving parts, and this is well illustrated by the various adjustments that had to be made just to make it possible to get material in and out of the yard. Immediate changes were needed on Twelfth Street and Broadway to facilitate access, and in June, the Louisville and Nashville Railway added a railway switch on and across Broadway for the same reason. Later that month, the Board of Works and Safety acted to ban parking along the six-street route that was used to get fabricated steel from International Steel's plant at Edgar and Tennessee Streets to the shipyard. The route had to avoid streets with sewers under them that might get damaged. Steel was moved from the plant to the yard twenty-four hours a day on specially built flatbed trailers, with each load being fifteen to seventeen feet wide and twenty-four feet long, weighing twenty-two to twenty-seven tons.[70] Some steel components were so big, however, that they required two of the trucks to move them—one moving forward and the other reversing, with their trailers pinned together.[71]

International Steel is itself a key part of the story of the Evansville Shipyard, from Walter G. Koch's pivotal role in bringing the yard to the city in early 1942 to the final delivery of fabricated steel for the 167th and last LST, launched in February 1945. For the company, it meant switching over from manufacturing structural steel and focusing instead on building sections of ships. According to the *Sunday Courier and Press* of October 25, 1942, "When International persuaded the Missouri Valley Bridge and Iron Company and its associates to move to Evansville to carry out its contracts for ocean-going ships, it also obligated itself to lend whatever assistance the shipyard might need in its operations…As the shipyard went into production, International went along with it, and finally turned into a boat building business." They invested half a million dollars reconfiguring the building and managed to borrow John Smith, assistant general superintendent of the

A section of LST about to be transported from International Steel on Tennessee Street to the Evansville Shipyard, 1942. *Willard Library.*

Interior of the International Steel plant, showing various steel parts coming together to make ship components, 1945. *Willard Library.*

Bethlehem Shipyard in Quincy, Massachusetts, as a consultant to help with the process of building ships. The demands of providing enough steel for the Evansville Shipyard were such that International ran out of space and expanded into an outside yard where the work continued for a time in the open air.

It should also be said that as well as providing steel for the shipyard and V-trestle piers and aluminum pontons for the Army Corps of Engineers, International also manufactured portable Bailey bridges, which were one of the most important pieces of equipment used by the Allies in World War II. In June 1943, the first bridge built in Evansville was actually assembled for testing by army engineers outside the plant on Tennessee Street. Thousands of these bridges, manufactured in several parts of the United States, would be erected all over Europe and the Pacific, often replacing bridges that had been damaged or destroyed by retreating Axis forces.[72] In September 1943, the British Royal Engineers' Colonel P.A. Clauson addressed a war bond rally at International Steel, observing, "This bridge you are now making has proved itself an excellent bridge of great flexibility…The Bailey Bridge is now the most important standard bridge for both American and British engineers."[73] And it was yet another way that Evansville helped to win the Second World War.

As the workers at International Steel toiled night and day to provide fabricated steel parts for the shipyard, workers at the yard itself were also working around the clock to turn that steel into ships. On Labor Day 1942, less than six months after the start of construction of the yard itself, the shipyard witnessed a brief ceremony marking the laying of keels 9 and 10, with eight other ships already under construction. Labor Day was the occasion for a national celebration of shipbuilding—over 150 navy ships were either launched or had their keels laid across the country. The theme observed nationwide was "Free Labor Will Win," with, according to the *Courier*, "ceremonies which [we]re intended to serve as an inspiration to all citizens and particularly to the more than 400,000 workers in more than 100 shipyards from coast to coast who are keeping production of US naval vessels ahead of schedule."[74] In many parts of the country, however, work continued as normal that Labor Day—as the *Evansville Press* of September 7, 1942, dramatically put it, "America, the arsenal of democracy, beat its ploughshares into weapons Monday on its first wartime Labor Day in 24 years. Workers in vital war production plants maintained full schedules in turning out the machines to fight the Axis and, in many cases, donated their earnings to buy war bonds." Full work schedules were also maintained in

International Steel workers assemble a Bailey bridge outside the plant on Tennessee Street, June 1943. *Willard Library.*

Evansville; the keel laying was informal with no interruption of normal work, and the yard's general manager, Frank Harrison, said, "We think it more fitting to proceed with work as usual, and this meets with the approval of the men."[75]

This initial surge of focused energy reached its climax on October 31, 1942, when the first ship was launched from the Evansville Shipyard. As the *Evansville Press* described, "The first ocean vessel ever built in Evansville hit the water at 12.20 pm Saturday...The launching was witnessed at close range by civic leaders, industrial executives and shipyard workers and their families, and from greater distance by additional hundreds gathered on the crest of Reitz Hill and the downtown riverfront." Bernie Horn, of Patronville, Indiana, remembered fifty years later "the awfulest crowd of people you ever saw. The workers were hanging all over the scaffolds and everything."[76] Admission was by ticket only, and the usual plant protection officers were backed up by plainclothes officers who maintained close observation of guests who had cameras. The steel launching ways, lubricated with paraffin, only allowed LST 157 to inch slowly down toward the river, and it took about twenty minutes to travel the one hundred feet. According to a letter that appeared in the shipyard monthly paper, the *Invader*, "The boat commenced to move slow…and down she went like a turtle chasing her shadow and not getting any place." As this was happening, the Evansville College choir sang the national anthem and then, as the ship entered the water, "Ol' Man River." As the letter writer concluded, "The old boat slid right in the water without nary a ripple and they rushed around and tied ropes to her and they tell me when she gets outfitted she will be out there helping to jab a jap or nock a natzi. Either way it's OK by me and I'm going out and buy another bond."[77]

In a memorable statement that in many ways summed up the perspective that people had on the Evansville Shipyard's role in the war, Captain DeWitt Redgrave, the navy's regional supervisor of shipbuilding who was a speaker at the launch, said:

> *Whether you realize it or not, you are right in the heart of this struggle. Because of the highly mechanized nature of this war, there is no clear*

A huge crowd starts to gather for the launch of the first ship—LST 157. Excited workers crowd the bow for a view of the spectacle. *Evansville Museum/EVPL.*

*distinction between working and fighting. The American worker in a war industry is fighting our battle for freedom as certainly as the blue jacket standing his watch in a convoy on the lonely, sub-infested North Atlantic…In this mechanical war the courage and valor of American seamen is an invaluable asset, but this courage will not be enough unless it is supported by the equipment which means the difference between success or failure in this struggle.*

Various other dignitaries spoke, and then Congressman Boehne mocked the Axis for underestimating America's "decadent democracy," saying, "The kind of picture we're witnessing today must be a revelation to him. His throne is tottering because men like you are producing results." Indiana governor Henry F. Schricker concluded the event with words of celebration but also of warning: "This type of craft is the spearhead of

A spectacular shot of men at work high above the Evansville Shipyard, tending to the cranes that made everything in the yard possible, June 1942. *Evansville Museum/EVPL.*

invasion…Everyone must work or fight. And if he does neither he is giving aid and comfort to the enemy."[78]

The results produced by the men and women of the shipyard continued, and LST 158 was launched just over two weeks later, on November 16, 1942. Five ships had been launched by December 7, the first anniversary of the attack on Pearl Harbor. The launch on that day was a particularly solemn occasion, with a thirty-second period of silent prayer during which thousands bowed their heads "in honor of the fighting men who have laid down their lives in battle."[79] February 1943 saw ten LSTs slipping into the Ohio River, including one remarkable period of five launches in one week that also featured two LST launchings on the same day. In the words of the *Evansville Courier* of February 22, "Just a year ago the shipyard site was a weed grown river bank dotted with squatters' shacks and beached houseboats. It was quickly transformed into a fighting unit of that phase of the war that is being fought on the home front—putting weapons into the hands of men on the firing line in the air, in the land and on the sea."

The transformation had been truly remarkable, but the work continued in three shifts for twenty-four hours a day, seven days a week, until the end of the war. People typically worked eight-hour shifts six days a week, but for about six weeks in April and May 1944, there was a push for twelve-hour shifts and seven-day work schedules. One welder recalled that their welding machines began to break down, and he said that one of the maintenance men told him that the machines could not go constantly without a break. After six weeks, they went back to six days of eight-hour shifts.[80] Roman Ritzert, who was chief hull inspector at the yard, remembered in 1992 that on the night shift, "it was as light as day…I'd look down at the shipyard and it looked like the sun was coming up."[81] The shipyard produced a total of 167 LSTs: 5 in 1942; 57 in 1943; and an almost-incredible 95 in 1944—approximately 1 ship every four days. It also built 10 up to February 1945. The last Evansville LST was launched on February 9, 1945, and at that point, the yard switched to making Amphibious Barracks Ships (APBs) and launched four of them. As Patrick Wathen observed, "The shipyard also manufactured 13 ammunition lighters and 17 oceangoing barges—201 ships total, costing $300 million. The output made it the largest inland producer of oceangoing ships."[82] All 10 Evansville LSTs that were lost during the war were destroyed by enemy action—not a single one was as a result of structural defects. In 1989, then eighty-five-year-old Roman Ritzert proudly said, "This bunch of country boys built good ships—ships that didn't sink."[83]

It is easy to imagine that the homefront was a safe place to be, and of course in comparison to the battlefield it was safer, but that is not to

The bow of hull one hundred is swung into place by two of the huge gantry cranes. It is decorated by unflattering caricatures of Tojo and Hitler, June 1944. *Evansville Museum/EVPL.*

say that it was a benign environment. The shipyard was a dirty, difficult, dangerous and, at times, deadly environment in which to work. James and Patricia Kellar set the scene:

> *A shipyard creates an always dangerous work environment. The brilliant flashes emanating from hundreds of arc welding devices threatened eyesight almost continuously. Laborers worked high above ground on scaffolds and*

42

*ship docks where a thoughtless step might result in a deadly fall. And those below were threatened by injury from plummeting tools and pieces of metal carelessly handled. The sound of their movement shrouded by the constant shipyard din, great gantry cranes endangered the unwary as they travelled, hoisted, and placed into position tons of steel. Heavily laden vehicles travelled on narrow congested roadways, ill-designed for their purpose, amid a welter of partially assembled components, welding leads, hoses, moveable storage buildings, and discarded junk scattered maze-like, impeding movement…If one problem plagued the Evansville yard more or less consistently throughout its history, it was in the effort to create a safe work environment.*[84]

Men and women were injured there fairly frequently, and men died, too. As early as December 28, 1941, an advertisement in the *Sunday Courier and Press* warned that industrial accidents would "impede defense production… [and] waste precious manpower that our nation cannot afford to spare."

These were to be prophetic words, in Evansville as well as almost everywhere else. The U.S. Maritime Commission Regional Construction Office conducted one of its surveys of the yard in April 1944, and it stressed the need for safety shoes and hard hats, observing that the availability of eight thousand safety hats had to be accompanied by "a strong sales campaign coupled with stringent rules requiring all employees working in and around ships on the ways and at the docks…to wear safety hats."[85] While most attention is paid to accidents, it should not be forgotten that infectious diseases could spread fast in environments like the shipyard. In March 1943, U.S. Public Health Services had to send two sanitary engineers to help launch a campaign against Vincent's disease, a respiratory ailment similar

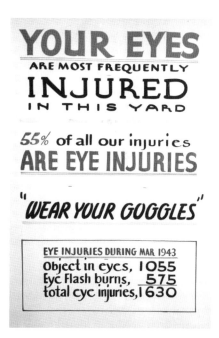

Safety poster hanging on a wall at the Evansville Shipyard. There were, on average, 1.8 disabling injuries every day at the yard. *Evansville Museum/EVPL.*

A group of workers gather around the scene of an accident at the yard. Judging by the faces, it was something serious, January 1943. *Evansville Museum/EVPL.*

to influenza. It spread rapidly in Evansville "due to unsanitary conditions in eating and drinking places, and much spitting in public places." Health director Dr. E.A. King said that the condition was "so prevalent at Evansville Shipyard that employees have dubbed it 'Shipyard distemper.'"[86]

It was, however, accidents that did the most damage. The first fatality came in September 1942, when James Massey died of a broken back sustained in a fall at the shipyard. In 2009, an eighty-five-year-old veteran of the shipyard recalled the incident as he toured the LST 325 Museum in Evansville: "The horrifying screams from the victim I can still hear, as they were drowned out amidst the tremendous ear-piercing clash from several metal chipping air hammers, and the throbbing vibration of the gantry-crane. The man fell some thirty-five feet to his death on the concrete below...I was only eighteen years old and was horrified by what I saw happen...Even to this day, its memory lingers with me."[87]

Massey was the first, but he would not be the last. In November, William Patton died after having had his skull fractured when struck by a piece of equipment.[88] In December, twenty-four-year-old Paul MacNeill was killed when a ship's steel plate slipped while being unloaded from a rail car. His companion Edward Perry suffered a broken collarbone in the same accident.[89] Just twelve days later, Jesse Carver, forty-six, was gruesomely killed when he was "mangled by [a] crane"; he was operating a jackhammer with a few others and so apparently did not hear the warning bell of the crane. He was dragged five feet before the crane could be stopped. His "left leg was torn from the socket and his right foot torn from the ankle."[90] April 1943 saw the death of Guy Abel after being struck by a bar that fell from a crane due to "defective material in the crane pulley."[91] Melvin Martin, rigger foreman of a gantry crane, was crushed to death between his crane and some equipment in October 1943.[92] Ten workers died in total from accidents in the yard, and from January 1943 to June 1945, there were at least 1,687 "disabling injuries."[93] That is over 56 disabling injuries per month, or on average about 1.8 per day, every day, for thirty months.

Numerous other shipyard workers were killed in auto accidents in and around Evansville (it is easy to forget that 137,000 Americans died in car accidents between 1941 and 1945[94]), and others were killed in other accidents of various kinds. One accident that took place just outside the shipyard and took the life of a man named Charles Owen has been vividly described by Clendel Williams. It is hard to imagine an incident that better captures the sense of expendability of workers in the pursuit of the lofty goals of wartime production than this one. Williams was on Ohio Street, waiting to clock in near the railroad tracks that ran down Ohio Street:

> *A freight train was headed west on the outer rails next to Ohio Street, clock alley #1 crossing. I was one of sixty some swing shift workers anxiously awaiting to clock in before the day shift came bowling out, knocking us down like a bunch of ten pins…As the caboose rolled past, the throng of workers pushed forward across the tracks unaware of an approaching train coming from the opposite direction on the second track. I was looking down so as not to step on the heels of the man in front when I heard screams…Someone had stepped into the front of the engine approaching on the second track. The cowcatcher flung a body off to the left clear of the tracks. Blood was splattered on several of the men who had missed being hit. The dead man was Charles Owen…As soon as the train had passed, the mass of workers, including myself, just as anxious as Charles had been, surged forward past his mangled body lying there. We all needed to get across the tracks and*

*clock in for our war production jobs. Someone would need to take Charles's place on the swing shift.*[95]

One horrifying detail that Williams omitted was that Owen's son was with him at the time and only "narrowly escaped the oncoming train" himself.[96]

The men who were injured or who died in Evansville's wartime industry were not, of course, alone. According to the U.S. Census Bureau, there were 94,600 total deaths and catastrophic injuries in American industry during the war years, while National Safety Council figures put the number of wartime factory deaths at 86,000. If the census numbers for wartime deaths, disabling injuries and injuries serious enough to lead to missed work are combined, the totals are absolutely staggering—over 2 million per year for a total that exceeds 11 million.[97] What is even more sobering about these numbers is that it can be said with absolute certainty that they underestimate the real toll—many of the numbers in the U.S. census tables, for example, have footnotes indicating that they are "based on fragmentary data" or "based on small sample sizes,"[98] and one scholar has referred to the process by which industrial accidents have been counted as "fatal subtraction" and "statistical MIAs."[99] During the war, this level of losses was regularly reported in the media, and it was soberly noted at the highest level, with President Roosevelt stating in 1942 that "among those who have been killed or disabled were men and women who could have helped to build planes, tanks, ships and guns—who could have served in civilian defense or in many other essential services."[100] The Office of War Information kept the public notified, with the *Evansville Press* reporting on January 20, 1944, that "accidents have killed 37,600 workers—5,000 more than announced combat losses of the armed forces—and have disabled 4,710,000 persons, or 60 times the number of men wounded or missing in action." The OWI observed that this was equivalent to the loss of 27 million workdays per year. In the pursuit of victory in a global war, it seems that this relentless carnage, in Evansville and everywhere else, was a price worth paying.

By the summer of 1945, the war in Europe had been won, and the end of the war in the Pacific was near. By early May, plans had been set for "Evansville Day"—a grand parade to celebrate the city's role in the war.[101] The event was to coincide with the launch of the USS *Vanderburgh*, the fourth and last of the four APBs constructed at the shipyard. But by the end of May, it was becoming clear that the writing was on the wall for the Evansville Shipyard, as the Missouri Valley Bridge and Iron Company turned its attention to another contract—managing a navy ship repair operation in Hawaii. The company diverted its senior supervisors from Evansville and

Six LSTs moored at the outfitting piers, where all the final work was done. Three have their iconic bow doors open, May 1943. *Evansville Museum/EVPL.*

offered jobs in Hawaii to the best of the workers.[102] The first 22 workers left the yard for Hawaii on July 6, with 75 more set to follow; it was expected that quotas would increase each week after that, and an "intensive campaign" was run to attract both current and former employees from the Evansville Shipyard. In August, with the end of the war, that contract was abruptly terminated, with some men still en route.[103] By that time, the payroll at the Evansville yard was down to fewer than 3,000; by September 5, the dwindling workforce of 1,700 heard that its last order was canceled. On September 25, the yard was declared to be surplus property by the navy.[104]

At the end of November, the *Evansville Courier* wrote, "Forty-four months of shipbuilding activities will come to a halt next week…[and] one of the nation's largest inland yards will become a ghost, haunting the banks of the Ohio River." A small group of workers remained, and the equipment that had built $300 million worth of ships lay either in neatly organized rows or "rumpled heaps."[105] There were various plans and proposals regarding the yard, but much of this was rendered moot on the freezing and windy night of January 26, 1946, when a significant part of the yard was destroyed in a fire.[106] Remaining property was sold by public sale in July 1946, and a few days later, the entire forty-four-acre site was put up for sale by the War Assets Administration.[107] Tons of records were preserved and stored offsite, but in December 1953, with the permission of the U.S. Bureau of Ships, they were burned. Today, almost nothing remains on the site, which has become a parking lot for the Mead Johnson corporation; the only physical remnants are some rusting parts of the fitting-out docks, which can still be seen jutting into the river, and one crane that sits incongruously in the parking lot of a local grain company. It is an ignominious end for what was a spectacular endeavor.

# 3
# THE OTHER INDUSTRIES

Although the Evansville Shipyard was by far the biggest employer in the city during the war—with a peak of over eighteen thousand workers in August 1944 and a total workforce estimated to be as high as seventy-thousand—there were many other significant contributions made by Evansville industry. A graphic contemporary illustration of this was the November 1942 Evansville War Products Exposition at the National Guard Armory. It was intended to give the local population a sense of what the city was doing, and as one local journalist explained:

> The exposition has been officially approved and is being promoted by the war and navy Departments as a workers' morale project. Though there have been other war products shows such as the travelling Chrysler exhibit shown only to Chrysler employees, the Evansville exposition is the first to display products of the various war industries within an entire city and be open to the general public. If it proves successful the Army and Navy will sponsor similar shows in other war production centers.[108]

It certainly did prove to be successful. With the Bosse High School band playing the national anthem and Mayor Dress cutting the ribbon, the *Evansville Courier* declared it to be "an immediate 'smash hit'":

> More than 6,000 men, women and children had jammed the huge Armory hall to see what Evansville in an industrial way is doing to aid the war

A curious and excited crowd surveys the exhibits in the War Products Exposition at the armory; at center is a ponton from International Steel. November 1942. *Willard Library.*

> *effort. For the first time, and probably the last, there is on display for the public exhibits from 19 Evansville industries of products which they are manufacturing for the war. And while pretty faces and shapely bodies are there in girls performing their daily tasks at the plants, it was cold, hard steel, brass, aluminum, thumping presses, hissing welding torches, and pounding air hammers that drew the great audience last night.*[109]

The exhibit gave a glimpse into the enormous variety of war materials being produced in Evansville. It included pieces of highly machined steel—secret and unlabeled—produced by the LaFendrich cigar company. Every ten minutes, a live machine gun fired bullets being made by the Evansville Ordnance Plant. Employees of Sunbeam Electric operated machines that made .45-caliber cartridges while a narrator explained the immense complexity of the processes "needed to produce bullets in vast quantities for hungry guns." Republic Aviation's display included "a 2000-horsepower air-cooled engine of the type that pulls the roaring

Thunderbolt plane into battle," as well as a smaller cut-away model of the engine to show off its internal engineering. Two of their plane wings towered over the display. A "searchlight revolves slowly, casting its ray upon industrial murals decorating the sides of the display room." Members of the state and city police as well as Coast Guards patrolled the space, ensuring that nobody was sketching or taking photographs. "In the Briggs Indiana display, girl riveters are assembling a portion of a plane wing before your eyes. Their tiny air-hammers pound the fasteners home as the crowd cranes to watch every step of the process." Hoosier Lamp and Stamping had representatives testing a bomb-tosser: "The little missiles come sailing down from a balcony and plunk heavily into a box of sand." The Cavalier Garment Corp showed off army clothes. "Mechanic Arts has a display of some of its classroom machinery being operated by students preparing for the day when they'll step into industry and make the tools of war and, later, the products of a new era of peace."

These female welders from the Evansville Shipyard were a popular attraction at the War Products Exposition at the armory, November 1942. *Evansville Museum/EVPL.*

Evansville College had a booth advertising the courses it offered for "training workers and fighters." Across the aisle from that was a twenty-five-man troop carrier manufactured by the Hercules Body Corporation and an Evansville Shipyard booth that featured welders and a steel-plate cutter as well as splicers showing how they made loops in steel and hemp ropes. Shane Manufacturing, National Furniture Company and Anchor Supply all demonstrated their products, including a canvas command tent that was said to look like "a small house with an entrance way." The Evansville Steel Scaffolding Company showed its product, as well as photographs of it being used while at the Faultless Caster booth, "a bevy of girls tests small parts that are unidentified." Two types of field stoves made by William R. Bootz were demonstrated, and in the center of the whole exhibit was a twenty-five-ton aluminum ponton from International Steel. The Servel exhibit included "plane wing construction, refrigeration units for military use, shells and a series of castings." In the large spaces on either side of the armory entrance were two temporary movie theaters where "continuous showings of actual war reels drew capacity houses all night long."[110]

The exposition only ran Thursday through Sunday, but it was a powerful symbol of the contribution that Evansville made during the war. It was hugely popular, with an estimated forty thousand people attending, and it included opportunities to apply for work in war plants and to buy war bonds. Taken as a whole, it demonstrated not just the wide range of war industries in Evansville but also the enthusiasm of the people of the city and the enormous number of products that were manufactured. This chapter will not enumerate every single one of the scores of items produced by at least forty-eight local companies but will instead look briefly at the contribution of several of the most important local industries in an attempt to convey the range and the vibrancy of Evansville's wartime contribution.

## Republic Aviation

After the shipyard, there is no doubt that Evansville's most famous contribution to the war effort was the manufacture of 6,670 P-47 Thunderbolt aircraft at the Republic Aviation plant located south of the city's airport. As has been seen already, the P-47 was an extremely important aircraft. Aircraft expert Mike Sharpe offered the view that "in service the 'Jug' (for Juggernaut) was a tough aircraft, able to soak up punishment and dish it out as well. It bore the brunt of early escort duties and was built in larger numbers than any other fighter ever acquired by the USAAC."[111] In a war of production like World War II, issues of scale and cost are important also: "More than 15,500 Thunderbolts were built, tallying the largest quantity of any American fighter…As Thunderbolt production accelerated, predictably, unit costs diminished. Up through 1941, the cost of a P-47 was put at $113,246. In 1942, this dropped to $105,594; by 1943 it averaged $104,258. For 1944, the unit price of a Thunderbolt was $85,578, and the following and final year of production, P-47 costs reached their lowest, averaging $83,001."[112]

But perhaps the last word on its effectiveness should come from Huntingburg, Indiana native Bill Mullen, who flew seventy-two P-47 missions—ten as bomber escort, sixty-two on close support missions. Its ruggedness, he said fifty years later, was its most important quality: "It would bring a pilot home after being hit. Pilots were real confident with it…The people of Evansville can be thanked for making strong airplanes."[113]

The coming of Republic, as has been seen, was announced in March 1942, with Hoffman Construction the contractor responsible for building

Four Republic P-47 Thunderbolts in flight. Evansville was to manufacture over 6,600 of these rugged airplanes. *Willard Library.*

the plant. The brick office building opened just two months and two days later. The rapid construction took its toll—there were injuries, as well as the first local civilian death as a result of the war. Elder Brooks, a fifty-six-year-old African American, was hit on the head by a steel hook: "The u-shaped hook, used for lifting tile, slipped off a crane under which he was working with another Negro, Melvin Piper, 22." In keeping with the segregated nature of life and death in 1940s Evansville, his death was announced under "Negro Deaths" in the *Evansville Courier*.[114]

Construction continued literally around the clock, and the plant was built with steel from International Steel. According to Diane Igleheart, whose husband, James, had worked with International before the war and was eventually its president, Republic Aviation had contacted various large steel companies, including Bethlehem Steel, looking for the availability of particular sizes of steel, but "International told them that if they would use what was in their yard at that time, they could do it very quickly." Even as the plant was being built around them, workers were already assembling the first planes to fly from Evansville, mostly from components shipped in from the Farmingdale plant: "As a suburban tract was transformed into a vast aircraft factory, Republic workers were putting together their first planes in garages, rented factory space, an abandoned office building and other out-of-the way locations. Through this program…the first Thunderbolt planes were ready for flight almost as the roof went on the main assembly building."[115]

In the words of Diane Igleheart, "they just kept building the plant around the way the plane had to go so when the last section that they built [was complete] the plane was there and it was sent right across."[116] On the occasion of the first plane—the *Hoosier Spirit*—taking off, Brigadier General A.W. Vanaman of the U.S. Army Air Forces told the assembled workers that "the rising tide of aeronautical armament in this country brings assurance of hard-won but certain victory to our nation and our allies." The P-47, he predicted, would "outfly and outfight" any other airplane.[117]

And within just over a year, incredibly, another 999 P-47s had been built in Evansville; the "one thousandth Thunderbolt was pushed out on the hanger apron just 20 months to the day from the time the first ground was broken for an airplane plant in a muddy, rain swept cornfield just north of Evansville." At the celebration of that milestone, Colonel Alonzo Drake of the U.S. Army Air Forces told a crowd of workers, "You have sent out 1000 answers to Hitler and Tojo and I can tell you these answers have been delivered." He then said that the creation of "the greatest air force in the world" in the United States was

Overview of the Republic Aviation plant. Airport runways are visible at the top, and Highway 41 is on the left. *Willard Library.*

*a miracle that surpasses anything that man has done before. It has amazed us; it has astounded our allies; it has thrown consternation into our enemies. The story of the creation of the new army air forces will make one of the most glorious chapters in American history. The miracle of the army air forces was made possible by millions of men and women like you in Evansville. Because of you, our fighting men have been able to move from the defensive to the offensive. Because of you, the flag again flies in the Aleutians; because of you our boys are now marching on Rome, and our bomber crews are giving the Nazis a terrible dose of their own medicine.*

Drake quoted a bomber officer who had participated in 138 missions of various kinds in hostile European skies. The officer had called the P-47 "the greatest plane of its kind in the world" and had said to him, "It is mighty comforting to look out and see those Thunderbolts flying along with us. I love the Thunderbolt. Give us more Thunderbolts and we'll do the job." Drake also said that though the Evansville workers had already sent one thousand answers, "the knockout answer has not yet been delivered and…Thunderbolt calling cards must be sent to Hitler in Berlin and to Tojo in Tokyo."[118]

The factory employed around five thousand workers, who were known as Raiders, with about half of them being women. It was a remarkably productive plant—it averaged 14 airplanes per day, but at times that number went up to 30. As James Harris has observed, "With 15.6 percent of Republic Aviation's personnel, the Indiana facility manufactured 39.8 percent of the total 15,683 Thunderbolts built."[119] Workers were constantly reminded of the high stakes by posters around the plant and by hyperbolic declarations, such as this one in the plant newspaper, *Republic Aviation News*:

> *With two fronts now, the Atlantic and the Pacific, calling for every Thunderbolt fighterplane that leaves the Hangar apron, Raiders of Republic's Indiana Division have given American fighting forces around the world their answer, straight from the production line…Enough P-47 Thunderbolts rolled off the lines at Republic's Evansville plant this past 30 days to turn the tide of a major battle, on either side of the world. Enough of the world's supreme fighting aircraft came out of Fuselage and Final Assembly and Hangar crews last month to protect inestimable numbers of Allied bombers from destruction…and thus save the lives of hundreds of American ground troops who would ultimately be given the assignment if aerial operations failed.[120]*

The plant continued producing airplanes at a remarkable rate—two thousand by May 1944, three thousand by August, four thousand by December, five thousand by March 1945 and six thousand by July.[121]

And then, abruptly, in mid-August 1945, it was over. The same day that the *Evansville Press* front page carried a story headlined "War-Weary World Enters Bright New Era of Peace," it broke the news that "Republic Aviation Corporation was notified all P-47 Thunderbolt work should stop at once."[122] One worker described what happened: "When we went to the plant, they told us not to report the next day, but to come back in two weeks for our separation papers and our last check. That was it."[123] The plant was offered for sale in September and was sold to the International Harvester Company in early 1946.[124] The only visible sign today that one of the most important war plants in America was in Evansville is a small blue marker located in the parking lot.

## CHRYSLER AND SUNBEAM

When the director of the Indiana War History Commission chose in 1955 to give examples of facts about the state's wartime industry that were "incredible," the first one that he gave was related to the Evansville Chrysler plant.[125] In 1941, the plant was producing 275 Plymouth cars daily, but by the end of the war, "They made more than three billion .45 caliber cartridges; almost half a billion .30 caliber cartridges; hundreds of thousands of rounds of other special types of ammunition; specially packed a billion and a half rounds of ammunition for use in the Pacific; reconditioned 1,662 General Sherman tanks; rebuilt 4,000 Army trucks; delivered 800,000 tank grouser and when the war ended, had just got underway on an order for 7,000,000 firebombs."[126]

It is an astonishing list of achievements, and what is just as astonishing is how quickly the conversion to war production happened. On June 30, 1942, test gunners fired the first rounds of .45 brass ammunition—since there was

Although Chrysler was chiefly involved in manufacturing ordnance, the plant also reconditioned Sherman tanks, here being tested on a special track. The track can still be driven on. *Willard Library.*

no ballistics building or proper testing range, they fired at steel sheets that had been hung in the coal house. This took place just ninety days after the conversion of the plant began.

But the very next day, due to a brass shortage, they were ordered by the government to make the radical switch from using brass to using steel—an enormously complicated challenge.[127] It was so complicated, in fact, that according to the Department of the Army, the .45 was "the only small arms cartridge fully converted to steel in World War II."[128] And it was so complicated that Chrysler did not have to do it alone: "Since its inception, early this century, the calibre .45 cartridge has been modified to improve its efficiency, but the most radical change yet made is now being developed. Since the Frankford Arsenal was busy developing other projects, three companies, Sunbeam, Chrysler, and Remington Arms, were asked to work together with the Arsenal experts to develop a steel cartridge case to replace the brass case used in the past."[129]

The Chrysler part of the Evansville Ordnance Plant, on Maxwell Avenue. The tank track was at top left, off Diamond Avenue. *Willard Library.*

Together, Sunbeam and Chrysler were known as the Evansville Ordnance Plant. Changing to steel was a long and frustrating process, as the characteristics of brass and steel are so different, and "all of the many problems of producing cartridges in large quantities had to be solved one by one."[130] Initially, Sunbeam tried to do it with the same steel that it had used to manufacture refrigerator domes, but in the words of its vice-president, J. Henry Shroeder, "This didn't quite do the job. So other steels were tested."[131] By March 1943, the new system was working so well that Secretary of War Henry Stimson credited the Evansville Ordnance Plant with perfecting the process and with saving a huge amount of brass for other efforts.[132] As George Blackburn has said, "In a single day this Evansville Ordnance works produced more .45 bullets than had been made by the entire American small arms industry in a year before the war. Chrysler not only made something it had never made before, but in producing steel instead of brass cartridges it 'undertook something entirely new to the small arms art.'"[133] In June 1943, when the two plants were receiving their Army-Navy "E" Awards for outstanding war production, the assembled Sunbeam workers were told that "General [Levin H.] Campbell, chief of ordnance, recently said that the development of the steel cased cartridge was one of the greatest mechanical achievements emerging from World War II."[134]

## SERVEL

The war saw Chrysler raise its workforce almost tenfold to a peak of 12,500, and another local company, Servel Incorporated, increased its employees from 4,382 to around 12,000 in 1944. Servel, a refrigerator manufacturer, had been Evansville's biggest employer in the mid-1930s, and its president, Louis Ruthenburg, was one of the most influential community leaders in the city and was a conspicuous and successful presence in the efforts of local leaders to get war contracts. On March 28, 1942, he was able to announce, "An additional war contract, totaling many millions of dollars, has been awarded to Servel, Inc. The new order eventually will bring about a substantial expansion of Servel employment…Servel, Inc. is currently working on various war contracts for the army and navy departments as both a prime contractor and sub-contractor. The new contract, however, will be much the largest it has booked since conversion to war production began."[135]

Several employees take a brief break to celebrate the 15,000th P-47 Thunderbolt wing panel assembled at the plant, October 1944. *Willard Library.*

In the end, Servel made wing panels for the Republic P-47s being produced in Evansville, as well as land mines and aircraft engine parts. It, like Chrysler and Sunbeam, was also in the ordnance-production business and manufactured 20 million 40-milimeter shell casings and 9 million 37-milimeter shell casings, as well as casings for other grades of shell, landing-gear assemblies, field ranges and airplane head castings.[136] It was a remarkably diverse output from a remarkably flexible plant, where both management and labor were able to make the difficult adjustments necessary to keep the war materials flowing. In the words of one historian, "virtually the entire plant was re-equipped and rearranged for…[war] production." During the Battle of the Bulge, it showed its ability to do this remarkably quickly: "Since cartridge storage cases were a critical army need during the Battle of the Bulge, the Evansville [Servel] plant achieved mass production on these cases within five weeks from the time blueprints and specifications were received."[137]

## CONCLUSION

While these four companies, along with International Steel and the Evansville Shipyard, played a gigantic role in Evansville's war effort and all six won the coveted Army-Navy "E" Award, in the end, another seven local companies would also win this award. The companies were Miller-Parrott Baking, Hercules, Thirwell-Henderson-Marine, Bootz Manufacturing, Hoosier Cardinal, Bucyrus-Erie and Holsclaw Brothers.[138] The meaning and significance of this award program was explained in the official government memo that announced its termination in 1945:

> *War workers in 4283 of the nation's top-flight war production facilities earned the Army-Navy "E" Award for their part in the defeat of the Axis Powers…Representing only 5 percent of the estimated war plants in the nation…[t]he Army-Navy "E" Award was granted only to facilities which were particularly outstanding in production for the War and Navy Departments. Excellence in quality and quantity of production were two of the determining factors in granting Awards.*[139]

For Evansville companies to garner thirteen of these is a remarkable testament to the quality and effectiveness of Evansville industry during the war, and it is fitting to conclude this chapter with words from the very last edition of the shipyard newspaper, the *Invader*:

One of the Army-Navy "E" Award flags about to be raised at the Evansville Shipyard. Thirteen local companies would receive at least one of these awards. *Evansville Museum/EVPL.*

*Evansville war plants met production quotas that brought amazing victories at Salerno, Anzio, Normandy, Leyte—on all the battle fronts. War industry after war industry in the city raised victory "E" flags…The splendid team work among civic organizations, labor unions, churches, and retail businessmen is in part responsible for "E" flags over Evansville plants, and battle pennants over tiny atolls in the Pacific…Evansville's part in the war effort will some day be written into the history of the state of Indiana and the nation. It will be a record in which all may be justly proud of having a part in the making.[140]*

# 4

# SOCIETY

The establishment of the largest inland shipyard in the United States [and] the location of a Republic Aviation Corporation plant in Evansville, superimposed upon an industrial city whose civilian plants had converted to the war program and who were already employing approximately 35,000 people, created problems of staggering proportions."[141] While these words of Gilmore H. Haynie, district manager of the Evansville War Production Board office, were certainly true, they did not tell the complete story. Evansville was definitely faced with problems, but it was also provided with opportunities, and this chapter will discuss both of these aspects. On the one hand, the war provided new prospects for African Americans and women and allowed the city to shine in the field of patriotic fundraising. On the other hand, old problems of racism and prostitution persisted, all of them exacerbated by the new challenges of wartime.

## RACE

The great Indiana historian James Madison has said that "racial prejudice was broad and deep in Indiana, and blacks faced discrimination in all areas of life. Many factories and nearly all skilled jobs were closed to blacks prior to 1941. The war changed this in large measure."[142] Madison explains that World War II had a definite positive impact on the status of African Americans:

*A new spirit developed as some white Hoosiers and most blacks saw the moral incongruities of fighting Nazism abroad while condoning racism at home. Perhaps more compelling for many whites was the simple fact that black Hoosiers were needed in uniform and in industry in order to win the war. By 1943 there was a severe manpower shortage that forced many formerly all white factories and businesses to hire black workers. Often these new workers faced discrimination on the job, especially in gaining access to skilled positions, but important economic gains were made during the war.*[143]

It is clear that the war had a very real impact, as thousands of African Americans in Indiana moved from "the roles of domestic servant and common laborer to that of highly skilled production line workers."[144] In Evansville, too, the "need for workers, and the ensuing prosperity that most enjoyed, cracked traditional stereotypes of the roles of African Americans...and established preconditions for change in the late 1950s."[145] In some plants, they were hired in large numbers, and both Chrysler and Sunbeam were lauded for their hiring by the president's Committee on Fair Employment Practice. In January 1944, for example, it was recorded that Chrysler had 1,186 African Americans out of a total workforce of 10,308 (11.5 percent), and by late 1944, that percentage had risen even higher. To put this in context, in February 1944, the Evansville Shipyard had 650 African American workers out of a total of 15,232 (4.3 percent), Republic Aviation had 100 out of 7,857 (1.3 percent) and Briggs had 40 out of 3,500 (1.1 percent). International Steel and Hoosier Lamp and Stamping employed none.[146]

For those African Americans who did get war work, however, the impact could be dramatic. Douglas Smith, looking back fifty years later, recalled how transformational his job at Chrysler was. He said that he earned "quite a bit. It was at a rate I'd never been before...It was paradise as far as opportunities were concerned." His wife, Lucy, also took a job at Chrysler and saw her income almost triple; she reported no problems and said of her white co-workers, "They didn't have time to be prejudiced." Judge Holbrook remembered in 1992 working as a riveter on airplane wings at Briggs where, he said, "I learned some skills that I probably would not have had an opportunity to acquire before."[147]

But the reality was that in most respects, Evansville remained a racially divided city in what was a segregated country and displayed what one historian called "the customs and traditions of a city that had always been essentially southern in outlook."[148] Most African Americans resided in a

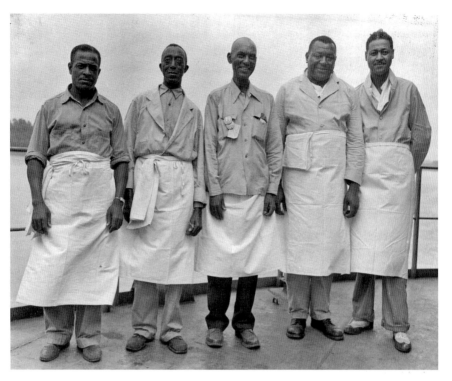

Five African Americans who worked as waiters at the Evansville Shipyard. *Evansville Museum/EVPL.*

segregated and run-down part of the city called Baptisttown, although a new public housing project, funded by the Public Works Administration—Lincoln Gardens—opened there in 1938.[149] According to local resident Talmadge Vick, interviewed in 2010, "Blacks were forced to live in segregated areas that were an eyesore and where the housing codes were not enforced. There were no African-Americans living east of South Kentucky Avenue. It took the open-housing ordinance [of 1968] to put an end to that."[150] Even where physical segregation was limited, issues could arise. In 1941, for example, the *Sunday Courier and Press* published a letter to the editor in which "a white American" apologized "to the two Negro ladies who were so humiliated by the treatment accorded them at the Coliseum Thursday evening. I refer to the two white ladies who refused to remain seated because two Negro ladies had the seats next to them. These Negro ladies were clean in appearance and had all the earmarks of respectability." The writer's solution, however, was to suggest that the venue "set aside a desirable section of seats for the colored people."[151] In the summer of 1944, two white college students were fined $100 each for "disorderly conduct" for not leaving the colored section of the Evansville Greyhound Bus station.[152] Interviewed in 1991, local man Judge Holbrook recalled the stark reality of this part of the country at the time: "I had a wife and little girl, but I enlisted. Blacks got [war] jobs but segregation didn't change. Coming home on furlough the bus stopped in Hopkinsville, Ky. When I returned to the bus the driver threw my duffle bag off and said, 'Nigger, you can't get back on.' I had to wait 8 or 9 hours for another bus."[153]

Camp Breckinridge, Kentucky, was only thirty miles away and housed up to forty thousand soldiers, including over two thousand African Americans. There were numerous problems for these soldiers in Evansville restaurants, hotels, shops and taxis. On one occasion, an Evansville restaurant refused to serve three African American soldiers, and the twenty white soldiers they were with walked out.[154] In 1943, tensions between white soldiers in Evansville and local African American youths culminated in violence and an effective lockdown of the city. The *New York Times* reported:

> *Military police patrolled Evansville streets tonight to enforce an out-of-bounds order for soldiers…to guard against outbreaks between soldiers and zoot-suited youths…The orders were issued after a series of incidents involving soldiers in the last ten days. City officials said several soldiers were beaten and robbed by zoot-suited Negroes. A Negro soldier and a white soldier were reported to have fired at each other. An Army paratroop lieutenant was seriously injured in a fight. "It is the unruliness of hotheads and smart alecs on both sides," a city official said.[155]*

Although that particular set of violent incidents was an extreme example, it is clear that African American soldiers routinely faced discrimination in Evansville. Darrel Bigham has said that "virtually all public accommodations" in the city were closed to them, and this included the USO. This led to the establishment of a center for them in Lincoln Gardens, run by a group of African American women and operated on voluntary work and donations. This became known as the Lincoln USO.[156]

And for Evansville workers, too, the racial divide remained stark. Except Sunbeam and Chrysler, local industries refused to upgrade African American workers, and even at Chrysler, there were strikes protesting the hiring of African Americans in 1943. According to the *Evansville Press*, "The dispute originated when about 50 white men walked off the job when some 15 white

An African American couple dances at the segregated shipyard picnic at Stockwell Woods, June 1944. *Evansville Museum/EVPL.*

girls in the department were replaced by Negro girls. Other departments walked out in sympathy."[157] At Briggs, the company generally refused to "upgrade" African American workers, and the only two women who were upgraded were returned to their original positions in the face of resistance, including a brief walkout, by whites.[158] At Republic Aviation, one female army inspector said later, "I can't remember working around any [African Americans] or seeing any in the area that I worked…They may have had janitorial jobs that I didn't know about…I don't remember that any of the army personnel were black."[159]

At the shipyard, African Americans were very much restricted to unskilled positions, with the vast majority being common yard laborers or janitors. Indeed, one of the shipyard's most potentially serious situations arose in March 1944 when rumors spread that three hundred African Americans were going to be brought in from the South to work as welders (a vital and highly skilled job). The fear that they would be employed at an equal level to whites led to a series of impassioned protest meetings and to the slogan "We don't work with them on an equal basis where we come from, and we're not going to do it here."[160] There were even dark suggestions that the "wide river right handy"[161] was a potential source of a solution to the problem—clearly a reference to lynching the African Americans by drowning. This was being said in a state that had in 1930 witnessed one of the most famous lynchings in American history.[162] After a period of heightened tension, however, the rumors died down and life continued as normal. That included a celebratory picnic for workers to mark the 100th keel in June 1944—or, more accurately, two celebratory picnics: one for whites at Burdette Park and another for African Americans at Stockwell Woods.

Over all, while some new opportunities did arise in Evansville for African Americans, it is the casual and routine level of racism and segregation that is perhaps most striking. To a significant extent, people of different races lived and died in separate worlds—they were educated at different schools, ate at different restaurants and fought in different regiments. Not even a cataclysm the size of World War II was going to change that.

# WOMEN

*Nearly half of the 11 million women employed in the United States in 1940 worked in low-paid, low-status clerical, sales, and service jobs. The 20 percent who worked in manufacturing were concentrated in a few low-paid industries such as textiles and garments. World War II substantially improved the economic prospects of women as the demand for labor to meet the nation's wartime needs exceeded the available supply of male labor and opened occupations formerly closed to them. Of the 18 million women employed in 1944, 36 percent held clerical, sales and service jobs, while the proportion employed in manufacturing had increased in relative terms to 34 percent. The entrance of over 3 million women into manufacturing represented a striking 140 percent increase over the figure for 1940, but the 460 percent increase in the number of women employed in male-dominated industries that converted to war production was even more dramatic.*[163]

For women throughout the country, World War II presented opportunities and challenges, and Evansville was no different. But although the war did not permanently change gender roles, it afforded Evansville women a glimpse into a different world. "I did a lot of overtime and swing shift work at the shipyard," one Evansville woman said. "Most of the time I worked below in the compartments where they put the beds [for the crew]. In the winter it was so cold in those rooms. They had shacks outside in the shipyard with pot-bellied stoves. You could pile into one of those and get warm. In the summer blowers blew air down to us. It would get so smoky we'd have to climb out."[164]

Some of the women who worked as three-position welders at the Evansville Shipyard, May 1943. *Evansville Museum/EVPL.*

In a sense, the war experience for Evansville women was like that—it was a new environment that they climbed into and stayed for a time, but ultimately they climbed back out. One example that illustrates this is the story of Emma Monroe, told here by Patrick Wathen:

> *The yard's first three-position welder—flat, horizontal, and vertical-overhead—was a woman, Emma Monroe of Oakland City, Ind. Her husband, Albert, started at the shipyard first, and she followed, getting her training first at Mechanic Arts and the shipyard school. "They had a call for everybody to go to work, so you went to work," Mrs. Monroe said. She welded for a year. "The foreman would bring people around to see my welds," she said. After a year, she began teaching in the shipyard school. She taught 200 men and women to weld. As a teacher, she made more money than her husband, but that caused no rift. "He was proud of me," she said. After the shipyard, Mrs. Monroe never held another job outside the home.[165]*

It has been estimated that women constituted about one-third of Indiana workers during the war, and in the state's war plants, they made up half the workforce by 1943. In Evansville, they were estimated to compose up to one-sixth of the Evansville Shipyard's workforce, about half of the five thousand workers at the Republic Aviation plant and an astounding 60 percent of the personnel at the Chrysler ordnance plant.[166] A federal report on Evansville from February 1943 observed, "In 39 selected establishments, 20,000 women are now employed out of a total employment of over 60,000, representing 34% of the total employment."[167] The same month, the *Sunday Courier and Press* published a special illustrated section on "Women at War" and introduced it with these words:

> *The butcher, the baker, the airplane maker…they are all women these days as the weaker sex has taken over many jobs formerly held exclusively by men. In the armed services as WAACS, WAVES, SPARS, and other kindred organizations, in war plants and shipyards as welders and mechanics…in civilian life in all type jobs, woman is doing her part. Ages range from 21 to 70, as the armed service girls and the Servel Grandmothers club shown here prove. The pictures on this page are a cross-section of the activities of the modern woman.[168]*

One of the women featured was Mildred Osmann of Newburgh, the only female member of the Boilermakers Union at the shipyard. She worked in

Not all female workers did nontraditional work; these women worked in the payroll department of the Evansville Shipyard. *Evansville Museum/EVPL.*

the yard's pattern shop, known as the mold loft, and had had to attend eight weeks of classes, three nights per week, in order to do so. Her two brothers also worked at the shipyard, and her husband was in the army. "Working in the mold loft is a lot of fun," said Osmann. "And I wouldn't trade back to my old stenographer's job even if it paid the same salary."

This edition of the newspaper also published for the first time what has become an iconic Evansville photograph, depicting the first woman to be employed at the shipyard as a welder, Evelyn Cox. Although there were many "Rosie the Riveters" at Republic Aviation, there were no riveters at the yard—all metal there was joined by welding. Cox was interviewed at length and described her job as a welder on Skid 3 as being a lot like dressmaking: "Of course, the forms we use don't look like the kind that grandma used to keep in the sewing room, but we do things with them that are like sewing. First after we lay out a pattern we tack it, which is very similar to basting. Then if everything is in order we go ahead and do the welding work, which is a permanent seam any way you look at it. And the best part of the whole thing is that working on my job isn't nearly as tiring as doing a day's ironing."

The article enthusiastically observed that "she has already proved how good a job women can do in what has for centuries been a man's field.

The shipyard's first female welder, Evelyn Cox: "My job isn't nearly as tiring as doing a day's ironing." *Evansville Museum/EVPL.*

Recently she was cited by the Shipyard War Production Committee for work over and above the call of duty…[T]hrough the entire winter she had worked without missing a shift and…every day she has done a better than average job." As a woman taking on a completely new role and identity, Evelyn Cox was extremely enthusiastic about her job at the shipyard:

> *This job is just like going on a picnic six days a week; it never gets boring. Several times a day I get to switch from one kind of work to another, and that makes it interesting. I think that the women who are waiting until Spring before applying for a job here are sissies. I just dress plenty warm in my long underwear and the weather doesn't bother me a bit. I guess the longies aren't very glamorous but they sure help when the thermometer drops around freezing.*[169]

As well as working for money, women in Evansville also volunteered in many different areas. Thousands of local women volunteered with the Red Cross, making tens of thousands of surgical dressings and operating the world-famous canteen that served an estimated 1.6 million servicemen as they passed through Evansville. It should be noted in passing that this was one of very few establishments in Evansville that catered to African Americans as well as whites.[170] Mary Ellen Emig worked at Sunbeam during the day and then put in a late-night shift at the canteen. Dora Hess Rawlings would work from 4:40 a.m. to 7:30 a.m. at the canteen and then go to her job as a teacher at Reitz High School. Fifty years later, she said, "I never thought I was tired. Today, I would complain loudly." Vivian Batteiger Holt's volunteer activity was to help young men write letters, often quite personal ones: "Sometimes they would be lonesome, and they said they didn't write too well, could I help. So, I helped them…It kind of made me feel sad because they wanted to be home with their wives or sweethearts."[171] And for Elise Strouse, the important part in her memory was that it was all free: "The canteen was just a nice thing to do. I remember a little sailor coming in with his change purse and asking how much it cost for a sandwich. When we said everything was free, he'd order up big and maybe even come back for seconds."[172] She recalled, years later, talking to a New York City cab driver; when he found out that she was from Evansville, "He turned around and said, 'You're the city that had that wonderful canteen.'"[173] Other women volunteered to dance at the USO. In 2003, then seventy-eight-year-old Dorothy Colbert estimated that she had danced with over two hundred servicemen at the club. She only wrote letters to a few of them and then stopped doing that when the deadly reality of war hit home: "I wrote to four or five, but after a while you ran out of things to talk about because we were only together for a few hours on that one night. One letter came back 'deceased' and I never did any more after that."[174]

For younger women, another opportunity to volunteer was with the Girls' Service Organization, which had 700 members by 1943. One of them was eighteen-year-old Jeanne Robinson, whose story is a powerful example of how deeply the war affected families in the city. She worked as an inspector at the Sunbeam ordnance plant, checking .45-caliber cartridge cases. Her brother Escoe Lloyd Robinson Jr. was a minister but had enlisted in the navy after Pearl Harbor. Their mother, Mary, also worked at Sunbeam, and their father worked at the shipyard as a welder, despite also being a minister who conducted church services in Boonville. The *Courier* reported that the "nucleus of Evansville's GSO was formed by groups of girls who had been organized at the YWCA and the YMCA for week-end soldier entertainment programs that preceded the USO and which are still being successfully carried out." On one particular night, their training class included 150 girls: 65 from

A group of servicemen line up outside the Evansville Red Cross Canteen, where thousands of volunteers served an estimated 1.6 million of them. *Evansville Museum/EVPL.*

A group of members of the Girls' Service Organization register at the Evansville USO. *Willard Library.*

Sunbeam, 32 from Hoosier Lamp, 28 from Lockyear's business college and 25 others. Other classes involved girls who worked at the shipyard. Training included instruction about clothing and "charm." To be in the GSO, a young woman had to be eighteen years old, or if seventeen, she had to have a job. All those who were under twenty-one needed parental permission. They participated in various dances and other forms of entertainment for the servicemen, and every week, groups of young women from the GSO went to Camp Breckinridge to entertain the men who were there.[175]

Welder Evelyn Cox's nine-year-old son, Melvin, would ask her every day when she got home, "How many ships did you build today, Mama?"[176] It is almost impossible to quantify how many more ships—and airplanes, bullets, shells, bridges, bandages and tanks—came out of Evansville because of the labor of women like Evelyn Cox and Mildred Osmann. As Mildred Harris said about female workers at Republic, "Men…didn't resent the women on the line because they knew they had to have them. They couldn't run that plant if all the women had been fired, or if they hadn't been willing to work. They had to have them."[177]

## PROSTITUTION

Evansville, like probably every other city in the world that was filled with soldiers and men who worked long hours in heavy industry, had serious problems during the war with prostitution, and no account of the city during World War II would be complete without some discussion of this topic.

According to the historian Max Cavnes, despite the fact that

> more than 75 of every 1,000 men called up for pre-induction physical examinations in the Evansville area during the early months of the war were found to be infected with syphilis…[s]trong objections were raised when the federal government suggested that Evansville's 250 professional prostitutes be driven from their homes. The mayor insisted that the federal government had no right to interfere since Evansville was not a defense area as yet and did not have a problem with soldiers as there were no army camps in the vicinity.[178]

The city was finally forced to close the red-light district in April 1942, when the commander of the Fifth Corps Area told the mayor that he had no choice. This zone of "commercialized prostitution"[179] was no small area—one federal report described it as "large, flourishing, and long-established,"[180] and in 1939, a police "investigation of conditions in the restricted red-light area on sections of North First and High Streets… reported…that there are 24 white establishments and two for Negroes."[181] There was a debate in Evansville, covered in the newspapers, between the majority of members of the Office of Civilian Defense who believed it was the best policy to close down the district and one member who "opposed the breaking up of the segregated area for prostitutes."[182] Fifty years later, the then police chief's son recalled that his father argued against the move since the prostitutes in the district were "screened for venereal disease by the health department"; with the red-light district closed, the prostitutes "wound up all over town," he recalled.[183]

The problem never really went away for the duration of the war. During this period, one resident recalled in 1987, Evansville was known as "a wild, wide-open town…Soldiers had money in their pockets and they were determined to spend it."[184] Camp Breckinridge sent seven to ten thousand servicemen into Evansville each week,[185] and while most of the time the blame for Evansville's prostitution problem was placed squarely on women, as was the case almost everywhere else, too,[186] on at least one occasion, a public official showed a refreshing willingness to hold men accountable. In October 1943, city judge James Crenshaw attacked servicemen who came to Evansville and "create[d] a demand for prostitution." He avowed that they were "as guilty of violating the law as the solicitors and the prostitutes. Just as patrons of a bootlegging establishment share guilt with the bootlegger." When asked in court if visiting servicemen created a market for prostitution in Evansville, beleaguered vice squad officer Wayne Berry said, "Yes, many of them are looking for girls."[187] And "girls" they often were. In late 1943, the city instituted a "crack down" on what the police referred to as "Little Casuals"—teenage girls who were engaging in sexual activities with soldiers.

But no sooner was this problem dealt with, through strict enforcement of a 10:00 p.m. curfew and harsher penalties for any adults involved, than a new problem arose in Evansville:

> *The war has grown a unique crop of "women of the evening," vice officers explain, who move from one camp town to another as police get hot on their trails. A wave of these camp followers has hit Evansville in the past few weeks and is giving Wayne Berry and Dan Hudson, members of the police vice squad, a new kind of headache…Experience with the law has made these women wary and wise in the ways of the police. Officers…who move about in plain clothes, are pointed out to new arrivals by the women who have been in town long enough to "know the ropes." "Pick-ups" are being made in taverns, on the streets, in bus and railway stations. So alertly do the women operate that with the approach of the officers, they disappear without any overt act that justifies their detention.*[188]

A specific example of this phenomenon occurred in April 1944, when a woman was arrested at Seventh and Main Streets at 1:15 a.m. with a group of soldiers; records showed that she had been arrested in Evansville in 1941, and subsequently in no fewer than six other places ranging from Georgia to Kentucky to Louisiana. She gave her name as Mary Bowley but had been known by at least seven other aliases.[189]

That summer, local and military police staged a crackdown on the city's parks, arresting over twenty women on one weekend in June. The women ranged in age from eighteen to forty-two, and all were examined at the venereal disease clinic. Dan Hudson of the vice squad said that, although the situation was a little better than it had been before, "there are still many promiscuous 'good time' girls and women who are endangering members of the armed forces by spreading disease."[190] In August 1944, Herman Folke,

Safety Board president, asked Chief of Police Freer to produce a plan to increase the size of the police vice squad. Freer said, "The detectives are worked to death now. I've got two men working with the MP's and there's two full-time officers and one part-time man at the rationing board." The problem, he said, was the wartime circumstance that "shoots 2000 soldiers in on us every week-end and sends in the girls that follow them."[191] Although two officers were subsequently added to the vice squad, it was never enough, and it was not until the war ended that the problem subsided; the red-light district was finally razed in an urban renewal program in 1960.

The prostitution situation in Evansville was considered serious enough to be monitored by the federal government all through the war; Janet S. Burgoon, regional social protection representative, wrote a stream of official reports on the city's battle with prostitution to the one-time "Untouchable" Eliot Ness, who was director of the Social Protection Division, Office of Community War Services. In April 1944, she said, "The problem in Evansville is one of promiscuous girls," but a detailed breakdown in December 1944 of the 2,308 reported contacts of Camp Breckinridge soldiers with prostitutes in Evansville from January to November indicated that promiscuous boys played their part, too. The report listed twenty-five different locations in the city where prostitutes were met. The most common place was on the street (979), followed by private homes (167), the bus station (153), the Blue Bar (119), Sunset Park (106), Beckerly's Bar (85), Oasis (84) and Bill's Grill (83).[192] And the problem was not just with soldiers. Burgoon's April 1944 report told a sad tale of a navy crew that came to man a newly completed LST:

> Recently a crew came to Evansville and was detained for a week to ten days. The men were housed over the USO which is near the railway station and were entirely without supervision for that length of time. Most of these men are quite young and straight out of boot training. By the time the boat was ready to be launched, it was found that a large percentage of the men were infected [with an STD] and the boat could not be sent until a new crew was assembled. As a result, crews are now brought to Crane, which is a hundred miles from Evansville and are kept there until the shipyard telephones that the boat is ready to sail. The men are brought in by bus and put right on the boat without a moment of liberty in Evansville. The Navy now anticipates no trouble.

The report concluded that Evansville was "very bad" and that "political factions" were "a very serious deterrent to good policing."[193] By 1944, according to the historian Max Cavnes, "Evansville, whose program had shown such hope in the early months of the war, had now earned the reputation of being 'one of the worst offenders in Indiana' with respect to the tolerance of conditions which bred venereal disease."[194] It was just one more way that World War II transformed the city.

## Fundraising

*Somewhere, on some far battlefield, one of our allies…one of our American boys…will fire a shot. It will be the last shot of this terrible war—the shot that brings Victory. That is the shot we are all hoping we are paying for when we buy War Bonds. Maybe it will be paid for thru a War Savings Stamp purchased by some child—it might be your child, or it might be that my children…will own the stamp that pays for this mighty bullet. Anyway, before this bullet is fired, many millions of others will be sent on their way, towards the enemies of civilization. So we must not stop buying War Bonds and War Savings Stamps, for each bit of ammunition, each piece of equipment, brings us that near to victory.*

So wrote singer and actress Lena Horne in Evansville's African American newspaper in September 1943.[195] And hyperbolic as this was, it was absolutely typical of the message that was hammered home to the people of Evansville every single day, in numerous ways, during the war. In the end, it was estimated that the people of the city purchased a staggering $150 million in war bonds and stamps.[196]

Between January and October 1942, for example, the papers gleefully reported that local residents had purchased "$6,532,033.85 worth of war bonds and stamps" but were still expected to do more: "During October, Uncle Sam expects people here to fish around in their billfolds, sugar bowls, and piggy banks and put $11,222,744 into war bonds. Chairman [Mike] Schaefer says it's a tough job, but he's sure that Evansville people will lay off fur coats a little longer and do a little more to help whip the Axis." Various groups helped: "The newsboys of the *Evansville Courier and Press* have done a huge job of house-to-house canvassing in the sale of war stamps. Since the start of the work by the newsies every purchaser of the Evansville papers has been approached on the matter of stamps…and the totals show that most of them bought." A women's organization set up a

A sign at the Evansville Shipyard shows impressive progress toward the established goals for the sixth war loan fundraising effort, 1944. *Evansville Museum/EVPL.*

telephone committee that "solicited the aid of every telephone subscriber in the Evansville phone directory."[197]

Most famously of all, perhaps, the movie megastars Abbott and Costello appeared in Evansville in August 1942 on a day of events that raised over half a million dollars and climaxed with a $1,000 war bond dinner at the McCurdy Hotel. It was reported that "Evansville bought $653,475 worth of war savings bonds and stamps Friday from two crackerjack, if zany, salesmen—Bud Abbott and Lou Costello...[who] said the total was the largest raised in one day for a city of this size. They were only in Evansville for six hours." The two comedians drove a ten-mile tour of the city and entertained at the Coliseum, including a version of perhaps their best-known skit—the "baseball rookie." For at least one Evansville family, it was an unforgettable day. Jeweler Jack Friedman was standing outside his store watching the parade when Costello beckoned him and, as he jogged beside the car, asked him if he could repair his broken watch. He said that he could, and Costello asked him to bring it to the McCurdy that night, later inviting his son Jimmy, too, who received an autographed photo of the duo.[198]

Outside the glamor of movie stars visiting Evansville was an almost daily grind of propaganda aimed at persuading people to part with their money for war bonds. A fairly typical example—a delightful piece of doggerel written by W.L. Miller of the shipyard fire department, entitled "Doing Our Part"—appeared in the shipyard newspaper of December 1942:

*United we stand, divided we fall,*
*If Japan wins the war*
*It will be hell for us all.*
*So buy bonds and stamps, make it a habit each day*
*And help put Germany and Japan away.*
*Let's rid the world of these troublesome pests,*
*Make our's a country of peace and rest.*
*Honor our boys on the battlefronts,*
*Sailors on the sea; submarines on the hunt.*
*Buying bonds and stamps will do this thing;*
*Let's all do our part. Let Freedom ring.*[199]

Despite W.L. Miller's many inadequacies as a poet, material like this clearly helped set the scene for prodigious fundraising. The shipyard was a conspicuous center of almost incredible levels of employee contribution—a payroll deduction plan led to 99 percent participation by October 1942. As James and Patricia Kellar have observed, "In 1943 shipyard employees purchased $3,500,000 in war bonds, equivalent to the cost of three LSTs. With the majority of shipyard workers earning no more than $1.20 per hour, this level of subscription is all the more remarkable."[200] Much the same could be said of Evansville workers in every other industry, as well as those who volunteered.

## CONCLUSION

While it is important not to overstate the positive and paint over the negative, it is clear that Evansville really did make a series of remarkable contributions to the war, raising vast amounts of money and elevating the position of women. The contribution of female volunteers alone was extraordinary, even if many of them had not also been going to their "day jobs" in the war effort. That all of this was done in a context of institutional and mostly unquestioned racism and alongside a flourishing prostitution industry that involved women and girls of all ages is another reminder that with an event of this scale, there are going to be many complexities in how we choose to remember it. The transformative impact of World War II on Evansville society was far from being an unambiguous positive; to remember it any other way is to distort history.

# HOUSING

On March 1, 1942, the *Sunday Courier and Press* said, "It is estimated that around 40,000 will be employed in our factories and, since this is roughly twice the normal number, a migration of staggering proportions into the city is indicated." Of all the many challenges that Evansville faced during the war, perhaps the greatest was the provision of housing for this "staggering migration" into the city. Without workers, not a single ship or airplane or bullet would have been manufactured in Evansville, but without adequate housing, there would have been no workers. The process by which Evansville came to have satisfactory accommodations for the thousands of new workers—and often their families—who flocked into the city is a remarkable and fascinating one. It was of course not without its flaws and its failures, but in the final analysis, it was successful.

Within days of the announcement of the coming of the Shipyard, it was clear that there would be a huge impact on housing. The *Evansville Courier* of February 24, 1942, reported that "urgent measures to meet an anticipated acute housing shortage were begun yesterday by C.B. Enlow, civilian defense director." A meeting was held the next day to confer with Earl Peters, the federal housing administrator for Indiana, and his staff. Judge John W. Spencer of the civilian defense council estimated that there would be ten thousand incomers by mid-May, twenty thousand by July and possibly forty thousand by the late fall.[201]

Three days later, it was announced that former Evansville city councilman John Koch was to lead a defense housing bureau. A block-by-

A Karl Kae Knecht cartoon discusses the challenges of housing the incoming flood of war workers. Bottom right, his signature elephant, "Kae," offers half a bed for rent, March 1942. *University of Evansville/EVPL.*

block survey headed by Judge Spencer had already begun to assess housing availability. In theory, a war worker would get a card from his employer, and then when this was presented to the bureau, he would get a list of available property. Brokers would get paid by clients, but workers would not get charged for the service. One member of the civilian defense council said, "Good housing for defense workers not only is our patriotic duty but it is our civic duty." Enlow warned about the likelihood of rising rents and said that if it got "out of hand that a 'fair rent committee' probably will be appointed."[202]

On the very same day, the *Evansville Press* reported plans for a two-hundred-home project near the National Guard armory on Rotherwood Avenue. The apartments were to be built by a newly formed company whose secretary, Theo Stein, said, "We had to act and act quickly. This is one part of the answer to the question whether Evansville is ready to handle the defense job." The cost was to be $500,000, financed through the Federal Housing Administration, and the whole project was expected to be completed by May 15. While some objections from local residents, including the adjacent Evansville College, were expected, it was thought that these objections would fade. The story concluded with the cheerful observation that "the apartments will be furnished with Servel refrigerators, gas stoves, built-in cabinets and sink."[203]

Less than three weeks later, preliminary work had just begun when ninety-one residents and property holders close to the armory filed a superior court petition for an injunction against further construction, claiming that it would be a nuisance. According to the *Evansville Press*, "It is charged that the apartments as planned 'are tenement building' having 'no architectural

The site of Evansville's first housing project in response to the influx of workers: the Armory Apartments off Rotherwood Avenue, March 1945. *Evansville Museum/EVPL.*

design'; [and] that they will be built without basements, laundries or garages."
The residents claimed to be as patriotic as anyone else and acknowledged
the urgent need for housing but believed that housing for workers should
be built somewhere else. Their lawyer said, "The proposed construction
does not conform with the neighborhood." Evansville College, despite also
having some objections to the project, was not one of the plaintiffs.[204] In the
end, there was a settlement that led to the project being more than halved
in size—it allowed for ninety-six apartments instead of two hundred—and
the building was all to be done north of the armory, effectively on the other
side of the armory from the objecting residents. At the end of March, work
began on the twelve eight-unit apartment buildings north of the armory;
preliminary work done to the south, suspended when court action began,
had to be removed. It is hard to imagine that class snobbery did not play
a role in this story—the houses to the south of the armory on streets like
Rotherwood and Runnymede are rather large, and it could have been
described as an affluent neighborhood in 1942; presumably the residents of
such a neighborhood did not want hundreds of poor working-class people
moving in nearby. It is not an edifying story and hardly an auspicious start to
Evansville's response to the housing challenge.[205]

Indeed, throughout 1942, the housing situation remained very volatile.
On August 5, the *Evansville Press* reported on the risk that the shipyard
would lose skilled workers because of the inadequacy of housing and trailer
facilities. A.B. Morris of the Missouri Valley Bridge and Iron Company and
Lieutenant L.J. Prues of the navy said, in what would become a frequently
heard refrain, "There have been numerous cases where trained men have
left the job for other locations where better housing or trailer facilities were
available," although it was acknowledged that constructing a trailer park
in what was called Pleasure Park on West Maryland Street had helped the
situation. Morris suggested that health and sanitation codes were restricting
trailer camp construction, and he questioned whether the trailers really
needed to have flush toilets—in some cases, he claimed, "trailer occupants
are better satisfied with conditions here than any place else they've lived."[206]

The following day, John A. Koch (who was by now the housing director for
the Evansville Shipyard) said, "There aren't enough homes for the workers
coming to Evansville, and trailers are the logical solution. It has been the
solution in other cities with big war contracts. We will have to provide for
these trailer homes, and until it is possible to bring the trailer parking lots
and camps up to the high standard of the county ordinance, we are going to
have to be lenient in enforcing these unimportant details."[207]

A housing unit in one of many trailer parks that sprang up in Evansville during the war, December 1943. *Evansville Museum/EVPL.*

The problem, he said, was that most rental properties did not allow children, but about 85 percent of war workers were married and most had children; he believed that many wanted to remain in trailers, in which they had invested as much as $2,000. Two large trailer camps started to develop. The one at Pleasure Park was expected to have space for 150 trailers by the time it was completed. By December 1943, it was said that "some 400 men, women and children live in trailers scattered over the 19-acre site. More than 90 per cent are employed at the shipyard."[208] The other large park was described as being at "the old city isolation camp grounds on Diamond Avenue off Highway 41 north." The operator had leased 60 acres from the city and was said to have acquired a license for 45 trailers, which could be increased depending on demand.[209]

There were eventually sixteen licensed trailer parks in Evansville, along with what James and Patricia Kellar call "an undetermined number of trailers…on unlicensed spaces throughout the community."[210] It seems that there were problems all over the city with getting a license due to flush toilet issues, and John A. Koch was very much in favor of relaxing that particular regulation. In August 1942, three war workers' wives, living at a small camp at 1221 East Riverside, complained about the fact that there was no license, and yet conditions there were such that "their present camp was the best they had lived in." As one young husband at that camp explained, "I have $1600 in the trailer. It is cleaner than any room or apartment we could afford. Our children have shade and grass and are healthier here than they would be downtown. I would suggest the county officer go about five blocks further out and clean up Villa Sites before he starts picking on a nice place like this. It is the best we have found in any city."[211]

Flushing toilets of a particular specification may not have been a matter of life and death, but the importance of regulation and inspection was graphically demonstrated on Christmas Eve 1943, when two children died in a fire at what was termed "Trailer City." The telephone had been locked away, delaying responses, and the *Evansville Press* reported that a safety inspection of the 103 trailers, 75 percent of which housed yard workers, revealed "many violations…especially in wiring. Shipyard officials agreed to cooperate in meeting recommendations for correction." Some four-gallon fire pumps were also moved to the park.[212]

The risks of unregulated trailer park life were demonstrated by a fatal fire at "Trailer City," December 1943. *Evansville Museum/EVPL.*

Issues with housing continued. In late 1942, representatives of the shipyard complained that "more than 200 valuable workers, recruited after wide search, have already left and others are leaving faster than replacements can be brought in." The same week, stories emerged about shipyard workers' families sleeping in their cars because of a lack of space.[213] In February 1943, John A. Koch said that the average immigrant worker traveled 60 to 70 miles to and from work, with some traveling as much as 150 miles per day. Koch said, "If the citizens of Evansville realized how much it means to the war effort, I believe they would rush to list their rooms and apartments with the War Housing Center, and more would take advantage of the government's offer to remodel their properties into living quarters for war workers." He also said that "as many as 20 men have quit in one day at the shipyard because of inadequate housing accommodation," while the yard's hull superintendent said that "about one third of the mechanics in his department had left and that all had complained about the housing situation here." D.E. Belt, who worked in the safety department, said, "I have a room in Evansville and my family lives in Mount Vernon, IL, 90 miles away. I've been looking for a place to live here with my family since November 2."[214]

At this point, things seemed desperate, but help was already on the way. In September 1942, the city council had created the Evansville Housing Authority, and Mayor Dress appointed to the board W.C. Bussing, Henry Bennighof, John Walton, William Rogers and M.K. Berman. Tasked with finding places to locate new housing, on October 9, they met with a variety of industrial and civic organizations and discussed the relative merits of several possible building sites. One week later, they signed a contract with the Federal Public Housing Authority, Region VI. The city decided to proceed with four federal housing sites of different sizes: twelve acres for the future "Fulton Square," seventeen acres for a site to be called "Parkholm," twenty-one acres for a project called "Dixie Manor" and twenty-six acres for what would be the biggest of the federal projects, "Gatewood Gardens." On January 22, 1943, bids were invited for the construction of the four housing projects; sixteen bids came in, and the Sherry Richards Company of Chicago was the lowest. The contract was signed on February 6, 1943.[215]

The *Sunday Courier and Press* of February 7, 1943, contained the stirring announcement:

> *A three-million dollar contract for 1,500 war housing units was signed yesterday by W.C. Bussing, chairman of the Evansville Housing Authority, with the Sherry Richards company of Chicago and the Federal Public*

*Housing Authority. Construction will start this week…"The prefabricated units which will be built at four different locations in Evansville's industrial area will go a long way towards relieving the housing situation here," Mr. Bussing said.*

Bussing explained that the homes would be prefabricated frame houses, which saved half a million dollars and could be built faster than standard houses and without the need to bring in masonry workers. The first project, which was due to be completed in ninety-five days, was on Shanklin between Fifth and Seventh Avenues. This was Fulton Square and would comprise 33 buildings, containing 276 units. The other three projects were due to be completed in less than four months. They were Parkholm, at West Maryland and Grove, with 40 buildings containing 324 units; Gatewood Gardens, at East Maryland and Kerth Avenue, with 61 buildings and 468 units; and Dixie Manor at Highway 41 and Morgan, which was to have

The Gatewood Gardens federal housing project under construction, 1943. *University of Southern Indiana.*

51 buildings with 432 housing units. All but Dixie Manor had "admin building, containing offices, community rooms, kitchens, maintenance rooms and storage spaces, as well as recreation grounds." These amenities, however, were to be added at Dixie Manor "at a later date." All units would have showers rather than bathtubs, and they were all strictly for war workers only.[216] On August 27, 1943, the Housing Authority adopted a resolution to "add an additional project for exclusive use of Negro in-migrant war workers. A site was selected between 2nd and 3rd Avenues north of Dresden Street to be known as Mill Terrace. This project comprises 50 trailers and 150 temporary housing units…Bids were opened October 29 for the Negro project and contract was signed Nov 16."[217]

The first shipment of the houses for the original four projects was expected to arrive in mid-March. Bussing sought to reassure anyone who was concerned about the future ramifications of this housing policy: "We wish to stress that these prefabricated, ready-made buildings, are temporary constructions intended to give shelter to migratory war workers cheaply and quickly. After the war is over and they are no longer needed, they will be disposed of…[T]hey will create no real estate problem after the war. When they have served their purpose they will be taken down and the buildings won't be an eye-sore to the community."

Due to wartime limitations, cheaper and "less stable" materials were used, and the actual cost of each unit ended up being less than $2,000, according to W.G. Schnute, executive director of the housing board. This price, incredibly, included "the landscaping, sidewalks, streets, curbs, gutters and sewage systems." As a result, Schnute said that the units would "not have the expensive and stable appearance of permanent dwellings." He said that "floors, walls and ceilings will be insulated and roofs will be of roofing paper and asphalt mopping. Interior walls will be of painted gypsum board and floors are of pre-finished oak. Space heaters, kitchen ranges, ice boxes, showers and complete plumbing facilities will also be included." All the officials stressed emphatically that these units were not going to be part of the Evansville landscape forever—the aim was to get them up quickly so workers would have places that were better than some of the places where they were currently living. Rain slowed construction, but the hope was that they would be erected as soon as they arrived—it took less than a day to set up a building, and some concrete piers were already in place at the four sites.[218]

A housing office soon opened to take applications. Leo Warren, the housing authority's legal advisor, said that the "houses will be occupied by persons who have been in Evansville less than a year and those workers who commute to Evansville from towns over 30 miles away. Persons living in trailers will also be encouraged to live in the new units."[219] Rent was based on income—someone who made over $1,800 a year paid between $24.25 and $31.75 per month; if you earned under $1,800, your rent would be between $20.75 and $23.75. All rents were dependent on the size of the unit and were inclusive of electricity and water. If the unit included basic furniture, which 340 of the units did, there was an extra monthly charge of between $3.50 and $6.00. There was to be no discrimination for "religious, political or other affiliations," but in a racially segregated city like Evansville, racial discrimination was accepted as a matter of routine. Preference for the units was given to "indispensable in-migrant civilian war workers and their families," followed by resident war workers who needed it; single people were excluded. And the sites were all, of course, selected to be close to war plants "for convenience of workers and to help ease the transportation problem."[220]

The whole housing situation was exacerbated because in the spring of 1943, there was virtually no building of private homes in Evansville due to a lack of workers and materials. The only construction that was going ahead was federally controlled, and was exclusively for war workers—such as the four big federal projects. A few other houses were being built while others were being converted under a government conversion housing program through which federal funds were available for homeowners to remodel their properties. In May, sixteen houses were being converted to house eighty-five families, but work was slow due to the lack of construction workers. And the needs were pressing—there had been one thousand recent applications from people seeking shelter. Mrs. James Welborn, the secretary of the War Housing Center, said that since March 1942, the housing division had made 1,500 units available, but she said that an urgent need persisted.

> *Some of the cases of applicants are pathetic. Many women are on the verge of tears as they ask for help in finding a place to live. One of our greatest problems is trying to discourage men from removing their families to Evansville before they have suitable living quarters…We have found families of eight and nine persons living in one room…If* [those with bigger houses] *would share a room or two, it would help to relieve the shortage. Conditions in defense plants areas are particularly bad. We have heard a number of cases where defense workers employed at night crawled into beds vacated a short time previous by day workers.*[221]

Mrs. Welborn might therefore be the first person responsible for putting on record one of Evansville's most cherished tales of the war years—the "hot bed" story—although she is certainly not the last, as it has been recounted numerous times over the past seven decades. Diane Igleheart said recently, "There were places where men slept for so many hours, then got out and someone else got in the bed…we called them 'hot sheet joints.'"[222]

Despite various construction delays, by June 1943, Fulton Square had its first lease signers, and by the Fourth of July, W.G. Schnute could optimistically claim that his survey of personnel departments at the city's war plants indicated that the housing demand would be satisfied when the construction was done. At Fulton Square, 129 units were currently ready, and of these, 53 were already leased and the other 76 would be leased within days.[223] The site was dedicated on July 15, and by the end of the month, a further 108 new units were available— 60 at Dixie Manor and 48 at Parkholm. All 276 units at Fulton Square were complete and "accepted."[224] Gatewood Gardens, the largest of the housing projects, was the last to open up, but its first 84 units were completed by October. The fact that it had not opened by September was probably just as well; the beginning of September brought the start of the 1943–44 school year and the genesis of yet another crisis for Evansville.

The *Evansville Press* of September 7, the first day of school, broke the story:

> School bells don't mean a thing to the residents of Dixie Manor and Gatewood Gardens, housing projects on US 41 north of the city and located in Knight Township beyond the city limits. The youngsters living there aren't in school. Neither township nor city schools are accepting them pending some definite understanding…City school offices, Knight Trustee Graddy, and even the county superintendent's office were besieged with telephone calls and some visits Tuesday from parents in the two government housing areas demanding to know where their children could enroll.[225]

Joe Graddy argued vehemently that since the Dixie Manor children lived in what he called "government tax-free property" they were "not a township obligation, and that schooling the children is up to the city." The city said that they were willing to take the children if the township agreed to pay for their tuition—as was the usual practice. The problem was that usual practice simply broke down due to the numbers involved. Vogel, the nearest school within the township, was so overcrowded that Oak Hill Club nearby had been "taken over as an auxiliary." The two nearest city schools, Howard Roosa

The Gatewood Gardens project, at East Maryland Street and Kerth Avenue, close to completion, 1943. *University of Southern Indiana.*

and Henry Reis, were already at capacity, so the federal project children would have to go to Columbia School by bus if they were to come to city schools. It was a disorganized and chaotic mess that would take some time to resolve.[226] At least for these children who were enjoying an unexpected extension of their summer vacation, the war had acquired a silver lining.

As days dragged on, the 250 children from Dixie Manor remained out of school. Charles Robinson, the county school superintendent, said, "There was a lack of foresight in providing school facilities when the housing units were constructed. We were not consulted. Now the matter is being dumped in our laps." Although the situation does seem to demonstrate a remarkable lack of planning, the episode also demonstrates again the novel problems that bureaucrats had to deal with. There was no blueprint for waging a total war of this scale in the mid-twentieth century, and city officials often had to make it up as they went along. In this case, there was even a question whether or not it was legal for the City of Evansville to educate children who lived in tax-exempt property. The city school board's attorney had ruled that they could legally educate the children, and a representative of the board said, "The board and its attorney took the position [that] education of the children is a part of Evansville's problem and that if it is held illegal to educate a child under the circumstances, board members are willing to assume the responsibility."[227]

Showing an impressive degree of flexibility and imagination, however, local officials continued to work on a solution. On September 14, it was reported that, following some informal meetings, Orvil R. Olmsted, regional director of the Federal Public Housing Authority in Chicago, had told them that "just as soon as the township trustees make application funds for the tuition and transportation of the students in question will be forthcoming." The press reported that this money would come from the Federal Public Works. This statement was followed by a conference in Indianapolis at the office of the state superintendent of public instruction to get his approval for using federal money for this purpose; Olmsted said that he had been told by Federal Public Works that they had $120,000 waiting for their applications and that it was a grant not a loan.[228] Three days later, it was announced that "city schools will be opened Monday to about 230 children living in Dixie Manor…A mutual agreement was reached under which transportation and tuition costs will be paid with federal money under the Lanham Act."[229] It seemed that the problem had been solved.

Unfortunately, on Tuesday, September 21, two weeks after the term had started, only thirty-nine children managed to get to school, as there was no bus to take them. Knight Trustee Graddy said, "Knight Township has no funds for buying buses and we will be forced to wait until federal funds are available." He said that it would be about ten weeks before they would be able to buy the buses. Some of the children who did get to school got there after they "hiked about a mile to the Walnut Street bus line and after reaching Eighth and Main Streets, transferred to the Mary Street bus which took them to within a block of the school." It took them more than an hour, and on arrival, they discovered that "no provisions have been made to provide hot lunches for the federal housing project children, and Mr. Lenon [Principal of Columbia] advised them to bring their own lunches until other arrangements could be worked out. There are a few places around where they could eat, but they are badly crowded."[230] At the beginning of December, federal funds still had not arrived for schooling, and though two Knight Township buses were being used to get the children to Columbia school, there was no transport to Wheeler School, where some of them were enrolled. Furthermore, there were problems in the afternoon, and they had to stay an extra hour before buses could get them. Finally, on December 10, the federal money arrived—over $40,000 for each of the townships—and Joe Graddy could buy another bus.[231]

Although the children were finally all in school, and much else had been achieved in providing accommodation, during 1944, the city continued to face the challenge of housing war workers. A large reason for this was that the Evansville Shipyard had its highest monthly employment levels of the war during 1944. During 1943, monthly averages ran at around 12,000 to 13,000, but in 1944, they rose steadily and from April were never lower than 16,700 with an August peak of 18,239.[232] In April, the Evansville Housing Authority added 185 more homes by approving a new twenty-eight-acre project located north of Diamond Avenue and east of North Kentucky Avenue, on the east side of the city and much closer to the Evansville Ordnance factories than to the shipyard. This was to be called "Diamond Villa" and was to consist of federal prefabricated homes brought from LaPorte, Indiana, where a planned ordnance plant had never been built.[233] This project would bring the total number of federal housing units managed by the EHA to 1,985. A further 100 mobile homes were brought from Flint, Michigan, to be erected on twenty-three separate lots, mostly on the West Side.[234] These were products of the Flint Palace Corporation and came fully equipped with "fixtures, plumbing and bath fixtures, and heating and cooking equipment. Some are without bedrooms and others have one, two and three bedrooms." Shipped by train to the Mead Johnson Terminal, they were trucked to their final Evansville destination.[235]

The housing crunch continued throughout 1944, with the former National Youth Administration center at Mesker Park being pressed into service in late July. In June, twenty days after D-day, Lieutenant A.F. Sweet of the Evansville Shipyard complained yet again that "workers are leaving the yard daily because they can find no homes for their families…skilled men cannot be found to replace them. Thus…the housing situation is affecting the production of LST landing craft so vitally in demand by the navy for the prosecution of the war."[236] The federal projects had very little available space, and what was available was not suitable—Lieutenant Sweet and John A. Koch had surveyed the projects in mid-June and said that they "found Parkholm 97.3% occupied; Fulton Square 98.2% full; Gatewood Gardens, practically 100% full, and Dixie Manor, 91.7% full." Of the 50 unoccupied units, 40 were what were termed "zero bedrooms"— unfurnished units that were designed for two single people—"which they said they had advised against before construction began. The projects all include two to three times as many zero units as larger units. With the loss

In the foreground is the Evansville Ordnance bullet loading plant, surrounded by the tank-testing track. Center right is the Diamond Villa housing project. *University of Southern Indiana.*

of younger men to the armed forces, the yard is employing mostly older men who have families." The last of the 100 mobile units from Flint became available in mid-June, and within days, "82 leases had been signed. [Sweet] said that more than 400 families have been waiting hopefully for the completion of these units and for the completion of Diamond Villa, a project of 185 prefabricated units now under construction." A further problem was the "serious tire situation," which made it difficult for shipyard workers since Diamond Villa was eight and a half miles from the yard, and one and a half miles from the nearest bus. At this point, 85 percent of the shipyard workforce had to drive or take a bus to work.[237]

And then, no sooner was the housing crisis here than it was gone, leaving in its wake a new conundrum—what to do with the now excess housing stock.

*War-jammed Evansville began yesterday to tussle with the problems of postwar housing. Federal and municipal representatives met to study disposal of some 1935 temporary housing units for families and nearly 500 single quarters for individuals...The day for removal of the five war housing projects must be carefully selected, both agreed. It must not be delayed to a time when the units would compete with privately owned rental properties nor must it be premature. If dismantled too soon the city will not be able to absorb the families forced to move.*[238]

The Diamond Villa housing project. Built to be disposed of after the war, these building are still in use in 2015, March 1945. *Evansville Museum/EVPL.*

That was the end of November 1944, and by April 1945, buildings began to close in Parkholm, Gatewood Gardens and Diamond Villa. In August, the *Evansville Press* reported, "What's to become of $6,000,000 worth of federal housing projects for war workers in Evansville, is the question facing Evansville Housing Authority now that the war is over. Theodore Lockyear, board attorney, today said housing authorities have two years after the war in which to liquidate projects."[239] In September, Dixie Manor and Gatewood Gardens were officially terminated, with their remaining residents moved out into other projects. Gradually, the other sites started to disappear, too, although the need to house returning veterans and potential future employees led to some delays, and much of the housing remained in place and in use for some years after the war. Gatewood Gardens, for example, was not finally vacant until 1959 and was razed in March 1960.[240] Almost incredibly, Diamond Villa still exists, and so does Fulton Square.

The Evansville housing challenge—and the schooling crisis that it involved—is a minor story in the great scheme of things. It might be seen as just one tiny blip in the middle of arguably the biggest and most complex event in human history. But it is a story worth telling because it illustrates the complexity of successfully waging total war. Not only did ships and planes and bullets and tanks have to be manufactured, but people—with their families—had to migrate to the cities where the factories were located, and once there, they had to be housed and someone had to organize an education for their children. Thousands of newly arrived workers had to be accommodated. On top of all that, funding had to be secured, responsibilities apportioned and, in the end, hundreds of children had to be safely transported to functioning schools, educated and fed during the school day and safely transported home. That Evansville was able to do all that—albeit with some stumbles along the way—is one more small but important testament to the city's remarkable ability to get the job done during World War II.

# 6

# THE DEAD

When Evansville's contribution to World War II is discussed, the focus is usually on the contribution made by the city's industrial plants, with most of the emphasis placed on the Evansville Shipyard, Republic Aviation and the Evansville Ordnance Plant. This book, perhaps, has been no different. What is less often discussed, and much less well remembered, is the fact that hundreds of local men who joined the armed services were killed during the war. In 1945, the *Evansville Courier* reported that the total number of local men who had been killed was 459. Their service, and their sacrifice, should not be forgotten.[241]

Stories in the local newspapers provide many interesting glimpses that provide a tiny piece of context for the men whose names are listed. The first Evansville man to die was nineteen-year-old Seaman Second Class George James Wilcox, who was killed at Pearl Harbor in December 1941—although it is worth noting that he was not officially declared dead until the navy released "Casualty List Number 1" in May 1942.[242] Oscar Steinback was believed to be the first Evansville Great War veteran to have a son killed in action in World War II, when his son, fighter pilot Lieutenant William Steinback, was killed in September 1943. As a boy, William had been a *Courier* carrier, and he had signed up after Pearl Harbor. Evansville's first African American military fatality was Private Rozell Bass, who died of wounds in North Africa in October 1942. Bass had been an outstanding football player at Lincoln High, and he was commemorated in Evansville by the Rozell Bass Post No. 1 American Veterans of World War II. His body was not returned home until May 1948. Sergeant Ray Muensterman, an infantryman, had been stationed in England prior to D-day. He had written home on June 1, 1944, telling his family that "he was leaving England and not to send any more packages for a while." Ten days later, Sergeant Muensterman was dead, killed in action in Normandy. His father died just three days later.[243] One of the saddest stories in terms of futility is that of Sergeant Hans Aabel, son of a prominent McCutchanville family, who was actually in a train on his way home in August 1945 when he accidentally shot himself with an Italian pistol while removing something from his bag. He was bringing the small-caliber revolver home as a souvenir.[244] Some local families made disproportionate contributions. Private First Class Arthur V. Zeller was killed in action on New Britain in January 1944; his brothers Clarence and Sylvester were both fighting in France, and Sylvester received a Purple Heart in August 1944.[245] Joseph Effinger was fighting with the army in France in May 1945 when his brother Aloysius, a marine rifleman, was killed on Okinawa in "his first time in combat."[246]

This book could easily be filled entirely with such stories, but space forces us to consider instead a small group of men whose deaths paint a fascinating and revealing picture—the students and alumni of Evansville College. There is no claim that these men are typical, or that they reflect the whole experience of Evansville. Indeed, in many ways, they are atypical. But they are an important subset of the Evansville war dead, and their experience tells us much about the American experience in World War II. This book

| | | | |
|---|---|---|---|
| J. LOREN BAILEY | '37 | JOHN W. McCONNELL, JR. | '43 |
| NEWELL R. BAILEY | '40 | DAVID MICHLOWITZ | '46 |
| JAMES R. BAIN | '44 | GEORGE W. MILLER | '46 |
| JOHN E. BAKER | '42 | ARTHUR F. PARKHURST | '46 |
| ROBERT H. BANK | '46 | DAVID L. RICHARDSON | '47 |
| JOHN W. BEYERS | '45 | CONRAD A. ROSE | '30 |
| EDWARD S. BLACKWELL | '41 | JACK W. STEMPER | '35 |
| ULESS B. CHANLEY | '45 | FRANCIS W. THEIS | '45 |
| ARTHUR DUGGINS | '46 | MAX K. THOMPSON, JR. | '41 |
| CHARLES W. DUNKIN | '40 | CHARLES A. WEBER | '41 |
| ALVIN JAMES EADES | '44 | GEORGE WIMSATT | '44 |
| BYRON W. ENGERT | '44 | EDGAR H. WITTMANN | '41 |
| CARL A. GRIMMELSSEN | '44 | HAROLD W. WOLF | '46 |
| ROBERT H. HEAD | '39 | HERMAN L. WOLFE | '46 |
| W. PAUL HOTTENSTEIN | '44 | DONALD H. WRIGHT | '44 |
| HARDIN C. KOFFITZ | '41 | PHILIP A. YOUNG | '46 |
| W. MAYNARD LIBBERT | '41 | | |

The names of the Evansville College war dead on the war memorial on campus. *Eilidh MacLeod.*

is being written on the campus of the University of Evansville, where a beautiful memorial every day reminds all who see it that the war profoundly affected the institution in ways both large and small. Hundreds of students and alumni of what was then Evansville College served in the armed forces of the United States, and thirty-three of these young men ended up dying in service. They were killed in many parts of the world in combat, and they died in many parts of the United States in accidents. Some were buried where they fell; others are buried back in Evansville. Some were outstanding students, some were star athletes, some were musicians and some were actors or writers. Some died heroic deaths that earned them posthumous medals, and others died ignominiously. All of their names are on the College War Memorial in the lobby of what is now the Schroeder Family School of Business, and it is certainly a place that rewards the spending of a few moments in reflection. As the memorial says so eloquently, "He lives in Fame that dies in virtue's Cause."

This chapter will discuss some of the Evansville College men who died, but in order to provide context it is worth talking briefly about Evansville College during the war. The college had been home to a strong antiwar sentiment in the years before 1941, which, according to longtime business manager of the college and its first historian Ralph Olmsted, was partly lighthearted but "also expressed the cynicism of students about the state of the world, which already was preparing for another armed conflict less than twenty years after the Armistice of 1918." In February 1941, the college newspaper, the *Crescent*, contained a lead editorial that said, in the form of an open letter to President Roosevelt, "We do not desire to 'defend democracy all over the world' as you so vigorously propose…[W]e suspect that you mean defending Britain, since it is said that the sun never sets on the British flag." The author of these words was Max Thomson Jr.; the irony was that he would himself die in a bomber over Germany just three years later.[247] Such student attitudes changed instantly as the student body sat together in the auditorium listening to President Roosevelt's "Day of Infamy" address, and the *Crescent* editorial of December 12 spelled that out:

*We did not provoke war. Let it be said we clung to the last thread of hope down to the last moment, down to the moment war was declared upon us. Let it be said we entered the war to protect our right to live…that we entered through our altruistic desire to smash the shackles from conquered nations, to restore God to the Godless, to re-establish order and security so that man may live to build, not to destroy. OURS IS A JUST CAUSE.*[248]

Exactly one month later, college president Lincoln B. Hale wrote an address to the college community that was stark and in many ways remarkable. He began by saying that "business as usual" was not an option and that "we face a radical readjustment of life. Now life must be lived with dedication to the high principle of service. Each one of us must make his or her contribution to the winning of the war and to the winning of the peace." The president then went on to say:

> Let there be no mistake about the issue. We are faced with a fight to the finish to maintain the principles of democracy which are fundamental to the way of life we have always known…The Axis attack is a basic attack upon our liberty, our properties, and our lives. Hitler makes his appeal to all that is evil in human nature—selfishness, the sadistic streak, and greed. He exploits paganism and challenges the basic principles of our Christian faith…The forces arrayed against us are formidable. Germany and Japan have efficient war machines that _can_ defeat us…If they win, we shall become the slaves of a Nazi ordered society. In one gigantic struggle the forces of evil are pitted against the forces of good—paganism against Christianity, democracy against tyranny…If we are to win, the united efforts of all of us must be immediately mobilized. We must be ready to make great sacrifices. Life becomes a grim and serious business for each of us.[249]

These were extraordinary words worthy of the extraordinary times.

Although there is no evidence that these extraordinary words led directly to students joining the military, they must have been inspiring to young people facing an uncertain future. The first Evansville College students had been called up for service in January 1941 when 6 National Guard members reported for duty at Camp Shelby, Mississippi, and over the next few months, there was what President Hale called "a small but continuous flow of men into the armed service."[250] In the end, almost 1,000 Evansville College students and alumni would join the armed services, and they will be discussed further in a moment. But as well as providing almost 1,000 people who served, the college made several other important contributions during the war. From 1941 to 1945, it was a center for the War Management Training Program for training and upgrading workers at the Evansville defense plants—including, of course, Republic Aviation, Servel, Chrysler, the Evansville Shipyard and Sunbeam. There were 192 evening classes taught, with a total enrollment of 3,851; a smaller program that was focused on business management enrolled 1,111 students in 56

A defense engineering class in session at Evansville College. Thousands of students enrolled in various war-related courses, 1942. *University of Evansville.*

classes. The college also ran various pilot training programs in conjunction with the Civilian Aviation Authority, the army and the navy, and by the time this ended in 1944, 639 men had been trained to fly—many of whom went on to be wartime pilots.[251]

And, as has been said, hundreds of current and former students joined the military. The *Sunday Courier and Press* of June 25, 1944, carried an interesting story about the lengths to which the college went to keep in contact with them all.

> *More than 700 Evansville College graduates and former students scattered around the globe in the Army, Navy, and Marine Corps know what is happening at the college as well as the alumnus who lives within sight of the campus and perhaps better in the opinion of Ralph Olmsted, executive secretary of the college and secretary of the college alumni association…During the past school year Olmsted has directed a program which has resulted in the mailing of more than 25,000 pieces of mail*

*weighing a total of almost a ton to men in Italy, England, Africa, New
Guinea, Australia, Alaska and many other countries as well as to scores of
army camps and navy stations in the United States.*

Staff at the college mailed the *Crescent* each week to the whole list as
well as a weekly mimeographed letter signed individually by a professor
or officer of the college. Personal handwritten notes were added on about
three hundred of them each week. All of this was much valued, and it was
said that "scores of letters of appreciation" had been received on campus
by June 1944. It should be noted that Evansville College had only graduated
550 men by this point in its history, and 159 of them were in service, 97 as
officers. Olmsted had recorded that 552 out of 2,500 male former students
were in service with 166 of them commissioned as officers. He estimated
that as well as the over 700 alumni and former students that they knew to
be in service, there were 100 to 200 former students in service that they did
not know about. He noted that there were 15 women in service, too. By this
point, the college authorities knew that 9 had been killed, all but 1 of them in
airplane accidents; 3 were missing, and 2 were prisoners of war. All of these
numbers were to rise before the end of the war.

Of the thirty-three Evansville College men who died in World War II,
twenty (60 percent) were members of the U.S. Army Air Forces (USAAF),
and one was a navy pilot. This may seem surprisingly high, but it reflects

Some of the men who trained at Evansville College as navy pilots. In all, 639 men were
trained to fly at the college, 1943. *University of Evansville.*

the reality that men with college experience were much more likely to be in the USAAF than any other branch of service due to the complexity of the tasks that were required. Men with college experience were statistically more likely than not to score well on the army's aptitude test and be designated for the USAAF; this can be seen, for example, in 1943 when, according to the USAAF historians W.F. Craven and J.L. Cate, "over 41 per cent of the men falling into the two top classes, according to the Army General Classification Test, of those processed and assigned at reception centers went to the AAF."[252]

What is more surprising, perhaps, is that of the 20 Evansville College USAAF men who were killed, 14 of them were killed in airplane accidents, and 8 of these happened inside the United States. The one navy pilot was also killed in an air accident in the United States. These numbers, however, provide us with a powerful reminder of the immense dangers involved in turning a tiny peacetime air force into the biggest combat air force in the world in the course of just a few years. These numbers, as with so much else of the American war effort, are staggering. In 1937, the USAAF had 20,196 men, which was 11 percent of the U.S. Army's strength; by 1944, it had undergone more than a hundredfold increase to 2,372,292 men, or 31 percent of the entire manpower of the U.S. Army.[253] The growth in the number of airplanes is almost as remarkable. Between 1940 and 1945, the United States manufactured almost 300,000 airplanes, with almost sixteen times as many in 1944 as there were in 1940; in 1940, around 6,000 airplanes were built for the military. But in the words of Craven and Cate, "in 1944 it turned out more than 96,000 military planes…and these were generally much larger and much more complex than those of the earlier year."[254] Overall, the United States spent almost a quarter of its entire wartime munitions bill on airplanes and in 1944 built more airplanes than Germany, Japan and Great Britain combined. Quality was not always as high as it should have been, of course—Charles Lindbergh famously described an early version of the B-24 bomber as "the worst piece of metal aircraft construction I have ever seen"[255]—and as Anthony Mireles has elegantly put it, "the AAF was training thousands of pilots and crew to fly the thousands of newly produced airplanes, and the fatal accident rate went up accordingly."[256]

The results were truly startling:

*Throughout the war, the Army Air Forces suffered over 6,500 fatal accidents in the continental United States resulting in the loss of 7,114 airplanes and the death of 15,530 personnel. This was an average of ten deaths and nearly 40 accidents, fatal and non-fatal, a day. The Army Air Forces reached its peak for both training and accidents in 1943. That year the Army Air Forces suffered 2,268 fatal accidents that resulted in over 5,600 fatalities and over 2,500 aircraft damaged or destroyed. The situation was better in 1944 with a 14 percent drop in accidents compared with 1943. However, there were still nearly 2,000 fatal accidents and the death of 5,000 pilots and crew.*[257]

It is very easy to forget when we look at the names on a war memorial that not all of these men died in actual combat but that many of them died far away from the war zone, in training accidents. Mireles has said:

*During the Second World War, thousands of AAF fliers were killed and thousands of AAF aircraft were destroyed in what essentially amounted to a third air front over the continental United States. It is interesting to note that the AAF lost over 4,500 aircraft in actual combat against Japanese army and naval air forces, at the same time losing over 7,100 aircraft in the states while moving airplanes around and teaching people to fly…The thousands of largely forgotten AAF personnel that were killed while flying in the United States were unfortunate victims of the cataclysmic struggle that was World War II just as if they had been shot dead by a German or Japanese soldier on a battlefield. Their ultimate sacrifice and their tragic stories should be remembered.*[258]

And, of course, thousands of USAAF personnel were killed in accidents that occurred in combat zones—10,314 were killed in aircraft accidents, and a further 4,848 in other accidents outside the United States.[259]

The Second World War led to hundreds of thousands of American deaths, and these men died in a wide range of situations in thousands of different locations. It is obviously impossible to capture the full range of these circumstances in any reasonably sized book. But it is the hope of this author that by telling some of the stories of the Evansville College war dead, the range and scale of the American sacrifice in the war will indeed be remembered. It is to nine of these stories that we now turn.

The first Evansville College man to die was Lieutenant John Loren Bailey, who was killed in March 1942 in an accidental bomber crash near Pendleton, Oregon. He was a multisport athlete at Evansville College, playing tennis, football and basketball and had also been a *Courier* delivery boy. At his funeral at Trinity Methodist Church, Dr. T.H. Gallagher said, "He was willing to die for America, and he gave his life for America. That sacrifice means as much as though he died on foreign soil." He then said to Bailey's parents, "You have today presented to God a boy who is worthwhile." He was buried in Oak Hill Cemetery, with future Hall of Fame basketball coach Arad McCutchan serving as a pallbearer.[260]

His friend George Wimsatt was also killed in an accident when his army bomber crashed in Pennsylvania in December 1943. He had played for two years on the Evansville Memorial High School football team and two years as a lineman on the Evansville College Purple Aces football team. His college coach Bill Slyker said, "George was full of life, zip and vigor. He always had a twinkle in his eye and the sort of personality that made friends. He was a very popular boy with other members of the squad...George and Loren [Bailey] were similar types...both clean cut, fine boys who got a thrill out of living."[261]

Lieutenant John E. Baker was a tank commander, killed at the Battle of the Bulge in February 1945, although his death was not confirmed until a year later. He died in heroic circumstances, for which he won the Silver Star. The citation reads in part:

> *Leading his platoon of medium tanks in the advance of the infantry, Lieut Baker instilled determination and aggressiveness of high order in his men by his exemplary conduct. An overwhelming enemy counter-attack with Tiger tanks and infantry in superior numbers met our forces in an attempt to drive them out of the area. Realizing the grimness of the situation, this gallant officer elected to stay and hold the fierce attack, thereby allowing the infantry to withdraw to safety.[262]*

According to the *Evansville Courier* of January 9, 1946, "His tank exploded and burned. The heat was so intense that the vehicle was a complete loss and Lieut. Baker perished inside." He had been part of D-day with the 709th Tank Battalion, and he subsequently had an award named in his honor at Evansville College.

Charles W. "Bill" Dunkin, an intelligence officer in the USAAF, was killed in a plane crash in India. In July 1944, the *Evansville* Press said:

> *We find it hard to believe that Bill Dunkin is dead. Killed in an Army plane crash in India. In singling out one young man, or two or three, I'm not forgetting that every day we have reports of Evansville youngsters giving*

*Left*: Charles W. "Bill" Dunkin, an intelligence officer in the USAAF, killed in a plane crash in India in 1944. *University of Evansville.*

*Right*: Lieutenant John Loren Bailey, Evansville College's first casualty of the war, killed in a training accident in March 1942. *University of Evansville.*

*their all for their country. But often I do not know the boys and while I realize they leave a spot in their inner circle of relatives and friends as well as the community that never will be filled the full impact of the war doesn't manifest itself until someone you were well acquainted with appears in the casualty list…It is tough on a community to lose young men like Bill. To say nothing of the terrible loneliness of a proud mother. If it is any consolation to Bill's mother and his close relatives, he is a boy who will be long remembered.*

Alvin James Eades has certainly been "a boy…long remembered." Indeed, he may be the only one of the Evansville College dead whose name is known to students at the institution today, as what was the Music Listening Room in the old Union Building on campus contains a portrait and the statement that it is "given by Alvin Eades and family in memory of Alvin James Eades who gave his life at Saipan in 1944." He was a first lieutenant in the army and a veteran of several Pacific battles.

Robert H. Head was a radio technician with a USAAF bombing squadron, serving in England, North Africa and Italy. In July 1943, the *Evansville Press* proudly quoted from a letter he had written to the female volunteers who ran the Evansville Red Cross Canteen in which he said, "I was in England and heard so many fellows remark about the free canteen for soldiers in Evansville and then when I came to Africa I still hear about it. I hope you can keep up the good work, and hope you know how much all of the fellows appreciate it."[263] He closed by reminiscing about a return to his hometown: "Boy, oh boy, how I would like to haunt Hills hamburger joint, Jensens bowling alley, or the Trocadero [night club] for a few nights. Just give all the home town folks my best regards, and tell them if they can just keep up the home front, we can manage to keep up the Second Front." Sadly, Robert Head never saw Evansville again; after safely completing fifty combat missions, he died in an airplane accident in Italy in 1943.[264]

W. Maynard Libbert was a captain in the USAAF and was also killed in an airplane accident. He died in a crash at Waycross air force base, Georgia, in March 1944 "after having flown 90 combat missions in North Africa and Italy." Libbert had purchased an Arab signet ring from a North African street vendor and said, "I've never gone into battle without it." He had been awarded the Air Medal, three oak leaf clusters and the Distinguished Flying Cross and, like many seasoned veterans, was serving as an instructor for new pilots when he died in a collision, just two months after returning home.[265]

Max K. Thompson Jr. was the editor of the *Crescent* quoted earlier and served as a radio operator on a B-17 Flying Fortress. His bomb group—the 351st—flew strategic bombing missions from its English base at Polebrook, Northamptonshire. He went missing over Wust, Germany, on August 6, 1944, just a couple days after his first combat mission, and was officially declared dead a year later. He is buried with 5,322 other servicemen in the Ardennes American Cemetery in Neupre, Belgium.[266]

Donald H. Wright was the son of a World War I veteran and served in the USAAF as a pilot and flight commander of a pursuit squadron of Thunderbolts in England. He received the Air Medal for "meritorious service in aerial flight over enemy occupied continental Europe" and subsequently was awarded three Oak Leaf Clusters. He went missing over Germany in March 1944 when the tail of his Thunderbolt was shot off, but by April, it was confirmed that he was a prisoner of war. Letters from another POW confirmed that he was fine, having been held at the famous prison camp Stalag Luft 3. "He was getting enough to eat and enough to wear. Through the help of the Red Cross and the YMCA, the prisoners had access to books and athletic equipment." He was moved to Mossberg prison where, according to a letter he wrote home, "conditions were deplorable…It will be good to be home again where I won't have to cook over a waste paper fire." Wright came home safely, reenlisted and was killed in October 1945 in a plane crash on a routine flight with a trainee in Alabama.[267]

Before concluding this chapter, it is important to note that although we mark the Second World War as being an event that ended in September 1945 with the formal surrender of Japan aboard the USS *Mississippi* in Tokyo Bay, for the American dead of the war, the story does not end there. For those who were to remain buried at or close to where they fell, fourteen permanent American military cemeteries were created around the world. In the words of the American Battle Monuments Commission, "In addition to their landscaped grave areas and nonsectarian chapel, the World War II cemeteries contain sculpture, battle maps and narratives depicting the course of the war in the region, and visitor reception facilities."[268] Many of these sites are places of sublime beauty. Perhaps the most famous of them all is the Normandy American Military Cemetery above Omaha Beach, which was described very movingly in 1977 by *Evansville Courier* columnist Joe Aaron:

> They say it was undiluted hell on this stretch of beach that day—that few battles in all history have been so costly—and it was easy to imagine as we stood there looking out to sea. Behind us, lying beneath row upon row of white marble crosses, lie more than 9,000 victims of that day and of the days following, their graves within easy hearing of the sea as it invades the beach, then recedes to invade again…[They] lie in eternal sleep as the heroes they were.[269]

For the dead who were to be brought home, the journey was just beginning. "The first returns of World War II dead took place in the fall of 1947, six years after the attack at Pearl Harbor. Eventually, 171,000 of the roughly 280,000 identified remains were brought back to the U.S."[270] It was a colossal undertaking of immense complexity; as the Office of the Quartermaster General wrote in 1951:

> The return program of World War II was global in extent, embracing civilized areas that had been visited with the unparalleled devastation of

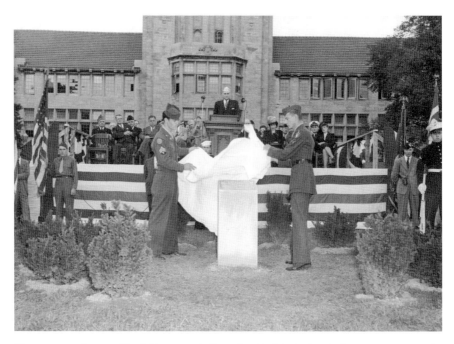

The campus of Evansville College was dedicated as the Vanderburgh County war memorial in September 1946. *University of Evansville.*

*total war, as well as vast land masses and remote islands where the most primitive conditions of life prevailed…In the opinion of the Memorial Division, "comparative costs were not the primary consideration in a matter so involved with sentiment." The Government of the United States, it held, accorded to relatives of the dead the right of decision concerning final disposition of their loved ones "as a final gesture of a grateful country to those who paid the supreme sacrifice."[271]*

Many Evansville families chose to have their dead returned to them, while others chose to leave the remains of their loved ones in the military cemeteries. In a 1946 editorial, the *Evansville Courier* said of the repatriation process:

*Foreign lands are soon to give up their dead of World War II for bereaved relatives who desire the remains returned to this country for burial…It is a hard job…This is a destruction of war that will never be repaired. The nation is doing what little it can to perpetuate the memories of those who gave their lives to keep the cruel conquerors from these shores. But that, little as it is, is all it can do for the boys and the men who made the supreme sacrifice.*[272]

The first ship bearing World War II dead arrived back in the United States at San Francisco in October 1947; the transport ship *Honda Knot* carried the remains of over three thousand Americans who had been killed in the Pacific war and was received with a ceremony that was described as "simple but impressively dignified."[273] It included what *Life* magazine called "a great green wreath sent by President Truman."[274] A photograph of the ceremony appeared on the front page of the *Evansville Press* the following day. The *Honda Knot*'s cargo included the first seven Evansville war dead to be repatriated, as well as sixteen others from the tri-state region. The *Evansville Press* reported that "the bodies of all but [one] are being taken to Distribution Center No. 6, Memphis General Depot…[The other] body is being taken to Distribution Center No. 8 Chicago Quartermaster's Depot, Chicago. From these points they will be taken on the final leg of the journey home—each body escorted by a guard of honor."[275] Even this small snippet gives a glimpse into the labyrinthine complexity of the process—and that was in many ways the simplest part of what was a daunting logistical and practical operation that covered the whole earth. The very last part of the process was the funeral, and in Evansville, the American Legion and the Veterans of Foreign Wars posts offered their services "to conduct military funerals when requested by the next of kin." An Evansville American Legion committee was set up to handle the arrangements, headed by the Adjutant of the Funkhouser post, and received such requests from several of the families.[276] Among those whose bodies were repatriated over the next few years were several of the Evansville College war dead (all those who were killed in accidents in the United States had already been buried). The remains of David Michlowitz came home in December 1947; those of Conrad Rose, Robert Bank, Alvin Eades, Robert Head and Charles (Bill) Dunkin arrived over the course of 1948; and Harold Wolf came home in May 1950.

By far, the most remarkable homecoming story of all the Evansville College war dead is that of Arthur Parkhurst, who had been listed as missing, later declared dead, after the loss of the troop transport plane he was flying near Tanauan Airfield on Leyte, Philippines, in March 1945. His body was not found, and his name is on the Tablets of the Missing at the Manila American Cemetery and Memorial. In 1989, however, the wreckage was discovered by a farmer, and the remains of the crew, including Second Lieutenant Parkhurst, were eventually recovered and

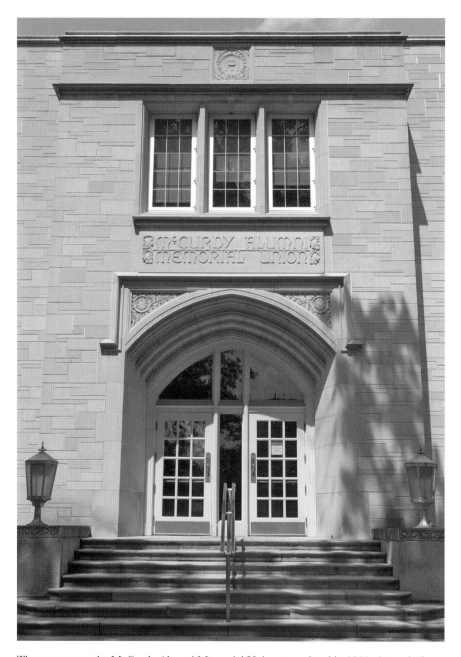

The entrance to the McCurdy Alumni Memorial Union, completed in 1951. At top is the crest of Evansville College. *Eilidh MacLeod.*

identified. The extraordinary story is told in a 2010 Defense Department news release, which is worth quoting at length:

> *The Department of Defense POW/Missing Personnel Office (DPMO)*
> *announced today that the remains of a serviceman, missing in action from*
> *World War II, have been identified and returned to his family for burial*
> *with full military honors. Army Air Forces 2nd Lt. Arthur F. Parkhurst, of*
> *Evansville, Ind., will be buried on Oct. 16 in Dayton, Ohio. On March 12,*
> *1945, Parkhurst and five other crew members aboard a C-47A Skytrain*
> *departed Tanauan Airfield on Leyte, Philippines, on a resupply mission to*
> *guerilla troops. Once cleared for takeoff there was no further communication*
> *between the aircrew and airfield operators. When the aircraft failed to return,*
> *a thorough search of an area ten miles on either side of the intended route*
> *was initiated. No evidence of the aircraft was found and the six men were*
> *presumed killed in action, their remains determined non-recoverable. In 1989,*
> *a Philippine national police officer contacted U.S. officials regarding a possible*
> *World War II–era aircraft crash near Leyte. Human remains, aircraft parts*
> *and artifacts—including an identification tag belonging to Parkhurst—were*
> *turned over to the local police, then to U.S. officials. Among other forensic*
> *identification tools and circumstantial evidence, scientists from the Joint POW/*
> *MIA Accounting Command used dental comparisons and the Armed Forces*
> *DNA Identification Laboratory used mitochondrial DNA—which matched*
> *that of Parkhurst's brother and sister—in the identification of his remains.*[277]

At the funeral, his nephew James said, "We missed so much, yet we have so much to celebrate and so much to be thankful for in his being returned to us. Welcome home, Arthur. Welcome home."[278]

It is, perhaps, fitting that the story of the Evansville dead—a story that began on a "Day of Infamy" in December 1941 with the death of the first Evansville man to die in the war—is a story that ended sixty-nine years later with the last of the Evansville College war dead being belatedly welcomed home. It is a powerful symbol of the fact that although the war ended in 1945, its effects have been felt for seven decades after. If someone were to spend a moment in quiet contemplation at the Evansville College war memorial today, they might well reflect on the awesome scale and complexity of the American war effort in World War II. They might consider how it helped to form the modern world. And they would be starkly reminded, of course, of its fearsome cost.

## Conclusion

On Saturday, June 23, 1945, the biggest crowd in the history of the city of Evansville—estimated to be around 150,000—assembled to celebrate "Evansville Day": "The parade was a patriotic pageant of red, white and blue beauty with more than 30 spectacular floats and a stunning array of armored might making their way down Main street...[It] was designed to pay tribute to the men and women from Vanderburgh county in the armed services and to laud the part workers and management had in war production here."

The parade, which was also intended to stimulate sales in the seventh war loan campaign, celebrated the commissioning of one of the last shipyard-built vessels, an APB named the USS *Vanderburgh*, and also featured an Evansville-built P-47 whose wings brushed over the heads of the packed crowd. Many other local contributors to the war effort were included—there were floats from Mesker Steel, International Steel, Hoosier Cardinal, Bucyrus-Erie, Bootz Manufacturing, Sunbeam, Sigeco, Servel, Shane Uniforms, Briggs and even Evansville College—and all of it was punctuated by martial music, marching military units, groups of veterans and heavy military hardware. The master of ceremonies was none other than Walter G. Koch.[279] In many ways, it was the perfect parade to mark the transformative impact of World War II on Evansville.

The war in Europe had ended on May 8, and the atomic bombs would fall on Hiroshima and Nagasaki six weeks later. The Second World War—called by John Keegan "the largest single event in human history"—was over. Arguably the largest single event in Evansville history was over, too.[280] The hope expressed in 1928 by President Harper of Evansville College that war would not visit Evansville for another one hundred years had been dashed. Hundreds of Evansville men had died in another war, and thousands more were wounded, damaged and broken. In June 1942, another president of Evansville College, Lincoln B. Hale, would say, "We are living in momentous times. Forces are at work which are shaking the foundations of our society. The civilization into which we were born is gone. In the fiery furnace of war's desolation, such as has never been seen before, a new era in man's destiny is taking shape."[281] A new era in the city's destiny had also taken shape, and while subjected to enormous challenges, it is clear that Evansville had risen to them and passed the test.

The keynote speaker at the "Evansville Day" banquet that June night at the McCurdy Hotel was John W. Snyder, the federal loan administrator

The biggest crowd in Evansville history assembled to mark "Evansville Day," watching a "patriotic pageant of red, white and blue," June 1945. *Willard Library.*

and future treasury secretary. He spoke eloquently and generously about Evansville's contribution to the war effort and evoked a ghost from the city's past:

> *Every resident of Evansville is entitled to feel the surge of satisfaction that follows a job well done—a job that has contributed its full share to the national accomplishment. Of this, your production of aircraft, tanks, trucks, mobile equipment, ships and ordnance is adequate evidence. Your civic leaders have exerted every effort to help Evansville do a commendable job. I am sure that Col. Hugh McGary, who founded your city back in 1812, would applaud, were he here tonight to behold your good work.*[282]

Snyder was confident that the city's founding father would have applauded what Evansville did during World War II; whether today's generation knows enough about that effort to applaud it is a different matter entirely.

The impact of World War II has been marked in various ways around the city over the succeeding seven decades. Having sent hundreds of its students and alumni to war, and having seen thirty-three of them die in service, on

September 26, 1946, the Evansville College campus "was dedicated as a living memorial to the men and women of Vanderburgh County who served in World War II."[283] The president of the college board of trustees commented at the memorial's dedication, "It is an inspiring thing that instead of a monument of cold stone and bronze, Vanderburgh county is dedicating a living, vital educational institution as its memorial to veterans of World War II."[284] In 1951, a new student union building on campus was dedicated as a memorial to those who served, and a fine brass marker in the lobby contains the names of the thirty-three men who died. In the late 1940s, a municipal Evansville war memorial was erected downtown at the Old Courthouse, bearing the names of the local war dead. Wonderfully, in 2005, a fully functioning LST took up permanent residence on the Ohio River in Evansville.[285] In early 2015, plans were announced for the Freedom Heritage Museum to be located very close to where Republic Aviation had been. And with the May 2015 passage of an Indiana law legalizing land-based gambling, the way was cleared for at least the beginning of the process that could bring the LST 325 to a prominent downtown site previously occupied by the Tropicana Casino.

But on the other hand, far too much of the city's World War II heritage has been lost or is almost invisible to the people of Evansville. It

The Evansville College war memorial, located inside the lobby of what was the McCurdy Alumni Memorial Union. *Eilidh MacLeod.*

is clear that nobody remembers that Evansville College was once "dedicated as a living memorial," and the original marker has long since disappeared. The McCurdy Alumni Memorial Union has been renamed and repurposed. The Eades Music Listening Room is now a videoconference room. A modest marker at what was once Republic Aviation and a small monument in the parking lot that was once the Evansville Shipyard barely do justice to the grandeur of the achievements that they seek to record. Other than a few skeletal pieces of steel and wood, and one decrepit rusting crane, there is nothing physically left of the shipyard. Grand old names from the

Returning veterans prepare to get on with their studies at Evansville College. Without the efforts of millions like them, the world would be a very different place, 1947. *University of Evansville.*

city's wartime production miracle—Sunbeam, International Steel, Servel, Chrysler, Briggs, Hoosier Cardinal and many others—are long gone from the city or remain in unrecognizable forms. Where fragments of the plants remain, there is no sign of their wartime role, and their massive contributions to the war effort go unmarked. With a few exceptions, the housing projects that sprang up in the city are long demolished. The two USO buildings, as well as almost all the hotels, bars, cafés and clubs where thousands of young men and women found entertainment are gone. And most importantly, the men and women who did it all—the labor, business and political leaders who brought the contracts here, the people who served in uniform and the workers who labored round the clock to produce the goods that won the most important war in human history—are almost all gone too. Barely a day goes by without the obituary pages of the *Evansville Courier and Press* recording the passing away of one or more of them. Before too long, that whole generation will have passed, and their stories will die with them.

It would certainly be great to see in the city an appropriately significant physical memorial to the people of Evansville whose monumental labors and sacrifice played such a vital role in winning the Second World War. It is long overdue but would be better late than never. But in one very important way, it could be argued that that memorial exists already. For without the efforts of these people—and millions of others like them—World War II would have been lost. Tyranny would have triumphed over freedom, and a new Dark Ages would have begun. If one is looking for the most appropriate memorial to the efforts of the people of Evansville during World War II, perhaps one need only contemplate the past seventy years of the history of the Free World.

# NOTES

## INTRODUCTION

1. *Courier*, November 12, 1928.
2. *Press*, November 12, 1928.
3. Leland, *American War and Military Operations Casualties*, 2. In 2015, the war was still considered the bloodiest in human history (Glenday, *Guinness World Records 2015*, 258).
4. Kennedy, *Freedom from Fear*, 14.
5. McCutchan, Lonnberg and Bartelt, *Evansville at the Bend*, 89; *Press*, May 17, 1944.
6. *Press*, September 23, 1941
7. Hewitt, "Role of the LST."
8. Quoted in Harrison, *Cross-Channel Attack*, 64.
9. Quoted in Clark, *Anzio*, 44.
10. Morgan, *Home Front Warriors*, 62.
11. Scutts, *Combat Legend*, 72.
12. Patterson and Perkins, *Thunderbolt*, 23.
13. Bigham, *Evansville*, 51.
14. *Sunday C&P*, October 25, 1942.
15. Stout, *Bullets by the Billion*, 2.
16. Blackburn, "Hoosier Arsenal," 313.
17. Quoted in *Press*, November 20, 1942.
18. Bigham, *Evansville Album*, 71.
19. Raymond A. Hoyer to Mark A. McCloskey, Federal Security Agency, August 25, 1943, National Archives, copy in Evansville Museum Archives.

20. Kennedy, *Freedom from Fear*, 322. Estimates for the number of Americans moving during the war go as high as 25 million. See Harris, "Rolling Bandages," 176.
21. Kennedy, *Freedom from Fear*, 230.
22. It was in fact a "joint venture"; the lead company was the Missouri Valley Bridge and Iron Company–Shipbuilding Division, but it also involved Winston Brothers, Haglin and Sons, Sollit Construction, Bechtel-McCone, W.A. Bechtel and H.C. Price—collectively called the "Joint Venturers."
23. Zeiler, *Annihilation*, 412.

## CHAPTER 1

24. *Courier*, August 30, 1992.
25. Ibid., March 16, 1941; *Press*, April 18, 1941.
26. *Courier*, July 4, 1941.
27. Ohly and Laurie, *Industrialists in Olive Drab*, 9; Finney, *Arsenal of Democracy*, 227. The OPM was established by Executive Order 8629 in January 1941. Among other things, it was designed "to formulate and execute measures to increase, coordinate, and regulate production of defense materials and to provide emergency plant facilities." In the summer of 1941, the OPM clearly had enormous power over the fates of American cities; in the words of Burnham Finney in 1941, "Of all defense operations, it immediately became the focal point."
28. *Press*, July 16, 1941.
29. *Indianapolis Star*, July 25, 1941.
30. *Press*, July 23, 1941.
31. *Courier*, September 2, 1941.
32. *Press*, September 9, 1941; September 10, 1941.
33. *Courier*, September 17, 1941.
34. Ibid.
35. Ibid., September 27, 1941.
36. Floyd B. Odlum to William Knudson, director general, OPM, October 7, 1941, National Archives, copy in Evansville Museum Archives.
37. Secretary of the Navy to William Knudson, director general, OPM, October 10, 1941, National Archives, copy in Evansville Museum Archives.
38. Hyde, *Arsenal of Democracy*, 19; *Sunday C&P*, January 18, 1942; *Sunbeams* 9, no. 18 (September, 1942), 1–2. Knudsen was the "first civilian ever to be named a Lieutenant General in the United States Army" in January

1942. In September 1942, he visited Evansville, saying at the Sunbeam plant, "Our boys in the front lines are fighting for you every day. You do the same back home."

39. Kellar and Kellar, *Evansville Shipyard*, 35–36.

40. *Press*, January 10, 1942.

41. Ibid., February 14, 1942; *Courier*, February 14, 1942.

42. *Press*, February 14, 1942; *Courier*, February 14, 1942.

43. McCutchan, Lonnberg and Bartelt, *Evansville at the Bend*, 89.

44. *Sunday C&P*, April 5, 1942.

45. Ibid.

46. Ibid., March 22, 1942.

47. *Press*, April 7, 1942.

48. Ibid., July 7, 1941. There was a sharp little squabble between representatives of the two sides at one of the early meetings of Mayor Dress's committee. For a wider context, see White, *Fragile Alliances*.

## CHAPTER 2

49. *Courier*, February 14, 1942.

50. Panicello, *Slow Moving Target*, 327. Jeffersonville had its own LST shipyard, building around ninety-five of them.

51. *Press*, February 14, 1942.

52. All quoted in *Press*, February 14, 1942.

53. "Story of the Evansville Shipyard," *Invader*.

54. Liberty Engineering Company, *Appraisal of Navy Department Property*.

55. *Sunday C&P*, October 25, 1942.

56. Clark, *Cornfield Shipyard*, 2.

57. *Press*, June 25, 1942.

58. Churchill, *Memoirs of the Second World War*, 410. He also said that shipping was "at once the stranglehold and sole foundation of our strategy." Quoted in Williams, *Battle of the Atlantic*, 113.

59. Keegan, *Second World War*, 118–19; Kitchen, *World in Flames*, 121–22; Lyons, *World War II*, 223; Doughty, *World War II*, 89–91.

60. Sulzberger, *World War II*, 95. There is an excellent map of the battle in Folly, *Palgrave Concise Historical Atlas*, Map 20.

61. Weinberg, *World at Arms*, 382.

62. Reynolds, *LST 325*, 120–26. Though it could be argued that by merely sailing across the ocean, they were part of the battle.

63. Kennedy, *Freedom from Fear*, 225.

64. *Sunday C&P*, October 25, 1942.

65. F.W. McWhiter to Frank Harrison, June 1942, National Archives, copy in Evansville Museum Archives.

66. *Press*, May 22, 1942.

67. Ibid., May 23, 1942. The "Home Front" column came with the instruction to "Clip Here and Mail to Someone in the Military."

68. *Courier*, August 30, 1992.

69. There has been speculation that a German spy operated in Evansville during the war, although direct evidence is limited. It is the backdrop to a series of novels by local author Mike Whicker.

70. *Press*, June 25 and June 26, 1942.

71. There is a photo of this in Morgan, *Home Front Warriors*, 128.

72. Sanders, "Push-Over Bridges."

73. Quoted in *Courier*, September 28, 1943.

74. Ibid., September 5, 1942.

75. *Press*, September 5, 1942.

76. *Courier*, August 30, 1992.

77. "I Saw the Launching," *Invader*, 6.

78. *Sunday C&P*, November 1, 1942. An image of the original Launch Program is in the shipyard's own publication: "Launching Program," *Invader*, 6–7.

79. *Press*, December 7, 1942.

80. Williams, *Echoes of Freedom*, 195–96.

81. *Courier*, August 30, 1992. Ritzert was the chief hull inspector at the shipyard and died in 1999.

82. Ibid.

83. *Press*, February 6, 1989. The precise fate of the ten Evansville LSTs that were lost is spelled out on the front page of the October 9, 1945 *Press*.

84. Kellar and Kellar, *Evansville Shipyard*, 170–71.

85. U.S. Maritime Commission Regional Construction Office, *Re-Survey of Missouri Valley Bridge and Iron Company*.

86. *Press*, March 16, 1943.

87. Williams, *Echoes of Freedom*, 281–83.

88. *Press*, November 16, 1942.

89. Ibid., December 15, 1942

90. *Sunday C&P*, December 27, 1942.

91. *Press*, April 10, 1943.

92. Ibid., October 1, 1943.

93. Kellar and Kellar, *Evansville Shipyard*, 173–76. The Kellars say that there were three deaths in 1942, when in fact there were four.

94. U.S. Department of Transportation, *Analysis of the Significant Decline in Motor Vehicle Traffic Fatalities*, 27.

95. Williams, *Echoes of Freedom*, 79–80.

96. *Press*, December 5, 1942.

97. Kersten, *Labor's Home Front*, 167–68. Numbers include prewar months of 1941 and postwar months of 1945.

98. United States Bureau of the Census, *Statistical*, 216, Table 238.

99. Linder, "Fatal Subtraction," 99. Industrial work has always been dangerous—as one veteran of the construction industry in Evansville recently said, "Risk had traditionally just been accepted as part of the job." Quoted in O'Connor, *Built Strong*, 58.

100. *Courier*, September 1, 1942.

101. *Sunday C&P*, May 13, 1945.

102. *Press*, May 29, 1945.

103. *Courier*, July 6 and August 18, 1945; *Press*, July 16, 1945.

104. *Courier*, September 5 and 25, 1945.

105. Ibid., November 29, 1945.

106. The scale of the fire is often overstated. Darrel Bigham, for example, said, "The biggest fire in the city's history destroyed it," (Bigham, "Evansville Economy," 26), but in fact, only four buildings were destroyed. Research in the National Archives indicates that the value of the loss was put at only $144,000 (Kellar and Kellar, *Evansville Shipyard*, 246).

107. *Sunday C&P*, July 14, 1946.

## CHAPTER 3

108. Ibid., November 15, 1942.

109. *Courier*, November 20, 1942.

110. *Press*, November 20, 1942.

111. Sharpe, *Aircraft of World War II*, 87.

112. Johnsen, *Republic P-47 Thunderbolt*, 34.

113. *Courier*, August 30, 1992.

114. *Press*, May 12, 1942; *Courier*, May 15, 1942.

115. *Press*, September 19, 1942.

116. Diane Igleheart, phone interview, Evansville, IN, May 20, 2015.

117. *Press*, September 19, 1942.

118. *Courier*, December 8, 1943.

119. Harris, "Rolling Bandages," 190–91.

120. *Republic Aviation News* 3, no. 9 (October, 1943), 1.

121. Morgan, *Home Front Warriors*, 62.

122. *Press*, August 15, 1945.

123. Harris, "Rolling Bandages," 191–92.

124. Morgan, *Home Front Warriors*, 62.

125. Turner, "Indiana in World War II," 5.

126. Stout, *Bullets by the Billion*, foreword.

127. Ibid., 20–23; Blackburn, "Hoosier Arsenal," 211–12.

128. Thomson *Ordnance Department*, 213.

129. *Sunbeams* 9, no. 19 (September 1942), 1.

130. Ibid., 4.

131. *Sunday C&P*, October 25, 1942.

132. *Press*, March 26, 1943.

133. Blackburn, "Hoosier Arsenal," 208.

134. *Courier*, June 17, 1943.

135. Ibid., March 28, 1942.

136. Morgan, *Home Front Heroes*, 194–95; *Invader* 3, no. 7 (May 1945).

137. Blackburn, "Hoosier Arsenal," 215, 449.

138. *Invader* 3, no. 7 (May, 1945), 3; *Press*, August 13, 1945.

139. The memo explained that other factors "included: (a) overcoming of production obstacles; (b) low rate of absenteeism; (c) avoidance of work stoppages; (d) maintenance of fair labor standards; (e) training of additional labor forces; (f) effective management; (g) record on accidents, health, sanitation, and plant protection: (h) utilization of sub-contracting facilities; (i) cooperation between management and labor as it affected production; and (j) conservation of critical and strategic materials" (Joint Army-Navy Release, *Army-Navy "E" Award Termination*).

140. *Invader* 3, no. 7 (May, 1945), 3.

## CHAPTER 4

141. Quoted in *Invader* 3, no. 7 (May 1945), 3.

142. Madison, *Indiana through Tradition and Change*, 384.

143. Madison, *Indiana Way*, 243.

144. Ayer, "Hoosier Labor," 98.

145. Bigham, "Evansville Economy," 29.

146. Information from the Fair Employment Practice Committee records in the National Archives, all cited in Kellar and Kellar, *Evansville Shipyard*, 149–51. See also Kersten, *Race, Jobs, and the War*, 68–69.
147. *Courier*, August 23, 1992.
148. Cavnes, *Hoosier Community at War*, 125.
149. Bigham, *We Ask Only a Fair Trial*, 219.
150. *Courier*, January 15, 2011. Vick was an outstanding citizen of Evansville as a coach, a teacher and a civil rights activist. He was also Evansville College's first (and only) African American quarterback. *Courier*, June 14, 2014; June 21, 2014.
151. *Sunday C&P*, February 2, 1941.
152. *Courier*, August 29, 1944.
153. Ibid., December 1, 1991.
154. White, *Fragile Alliances*, 121.
155. *New York Times*, June 28, 1943.
156. Bigham, *We Ask Only a Fair Trial*, 230–31.
157. *Press*, September 27, 1943.
158. White, *Fragile Alliances*, 121; Kellar and Kellar, *Evansville Shipyard*, 152.
159. Harris, "Rolling Bandages," 186.
160. Cavnes, *Hoosier Community*, 127.
161. Kellar and Kellar, *Evansville Shipyard*, 154.
162. The lynching of two black teenagers in Marion, Indiana, had been captured in an iconic and much-reproduced photograph. See Madison, *Lynching in the Heartland*.
163. Gabin, "Women Defense Workers," 106.
164. *Courier*, July 16, 2003.
165. Ibid., August 30, 1992.
166. Gabin, "Women Defense Workers," 109, 117; Kellar and Kellar, *Evansville Shipyard*, 163.
167. Federal Security Agency Office of Community War Services Region VI, *Report*, 5.
168. *Sunday C&P*, February 28, 1943.
169. Ibid.
170. Bigham, *We Ask Only a Fair Trial*, 230. The Willard Library in Evansville was also one of the few institutions in the city that served, in the words of its founder Willard Carpenter in 1876, "the people of all classes, races and sexes."
171. *Courier*, September 28, 1995.
172. Ibid., April 3, 2003.

173. Ibid., August 23, 1992.

174. Ibid., April 2, 2003.

175. Ibid., March 10, 1943.

176. *Sunday C&P*, February 28, 1943.

177. Harris, "Rolling Bandages," 182.

178. Cavnes, *Hoosier Community at War*, 225.

179. Office of Defense Health and Welfare Services, Region VI, *Report*, 11.

180. Federal Security Agency Office of Community War Services Region VI, *Report*, 20.

181. *Press*, April 29, 1939.

182. *Sunday C&P*, March 22, 1942.

183. *Courier*, December 1, 1991. Evansville before the war seems to have been a classic example of "situations where prostitution was prohibited by law but regulated in practice" (Ditmore, *Prostitution and Sex Work*), 53.

184. *Courier*, February 15, 1987.

185. Burgoon, *Memo to Eliot Ness*.

186. Hegarty, "Patriot or Prostitute?" 119. "The military spoke of 'moral suasion' in the same breath with prophylactics; soldiers insisted sex was here to stay, and sexualized women appeared as responsible both for maintaining morale and spreading venereal diseases. The authorities had found the 'enemy' and she was everywhere."

187. *Courier*, October 2, 1943. For a fascinating discussion of how the army dealt with sexually transmitted infections during World War II, see Coates, Hoff and Hoff, *Preventive Medicine*.

188. *Courier*, January 29, 1944. Wayne Berry was to serve as Evansville Police chief from 1945 to 1947.

189. Ibid., April 27, 1944.

190. Ibid., June 27, 1944.

191. *Press*, August 25, 1944.

192. Burgoon, *Memo to Eliot Ness*.

193. Ibid.

194. Cavnes, *Hoosier Community at War*, 227. He is quoting Burgoon.

195. *Evansville Argus*, September 24, 1943.

196. *Courier*, August 19, 1995.

197. *Sunday C&P*, October 25, 1942.

198. *Press*, August 15, 1942; *Sunday C&P*, August 16, 1942.

199. *Invader* 1, no. 3 (December 1942), 7.

200. Kellar and Kellar, *Evansville Shipyard*, 216.

## CHAPTER 5

201. *Courier*, February 24, 1942. The Vanderburgh Civilian Defense Council had been set up in January 1942, with C.B. Enlow as director and Judge Spencer as vice-chairman. The council was divided into six areas, covering public works and safety; civilian protection; civilian economy; financial activities; agriculture and industry; and educational, religious and civic organizations (*Courier*, January 9, 1942).

202. *Press*, February 27, 1942.

203. Ibid. Coincidentally, Louis Ruthenburg, President of Servel, was vice-chairman of the Vanderburgh Civilian Defense Council.

204. *Press*, March 10, 1942.

205. Ibid., March 27 and 28, 1942; *Courier*, March 22, 1942.

206. *Press*, August 5, 1942.

207. Van Ells, *To Hear Only Thunder Again*, 212. Evansville, of course, was not alone in having to face this challenge: "According to one estimate, fully one in eight war workers had been housed in a trailer at some point during the war."

208. *Courier*, December 29, 1943.

209. Ibid., August 6, 1942.

210. Kellar and Kellar, *Evansville Shipyard*, 224.

211. *Courier*, August 6, 1942.

212. *Press*, January 6, 1944; December 29, 1943.

213. *Courier*, November 17, 1942; *Press*, November 20, 1942.

214. *Courier*, February 24, 1943.

215. *Sunday C&P*, February 6, 1944.

216. Ibid., February 7, 1943.

217. Ibid., February 6, 1944. Classified advertisements in the local press referred to "Mill Terrace Colored Housing." The land was leased from the Igleheart Milling Company (*Sunday C&P*, October 10, 1943).

218. *Sunday C&P*, March 21, 1943.

219. Ibid.

220. *Press*, April 17, 1943.

221. Ibid., May 3, 1943.

222. Mrs. Igleheart also mentioned cabins at the corner of Petersburg Road and Highway 41 that were so called "for entirely different reasons." (Igleheart, phone interview). "Hot beds" were also mentioned recently by Thomas Lonnberg, director of history at the Evansville Museum of Arts, History and Science on WNIN TV ("World War Two and the LST

Shipyard). See also: *Press*, April 19, 1977; Bigham, *Evansville*, 81. One person who experienced this was columnist Bish Thompson, who spoke of "renting a 'hot bed' at the YMCA. He shared the bed with two others who slept in shifts each day." (*Sunday C&P*, September 1, 1974.)

223. *Sunday C&P*, July 4, 1943.
224. *Press*, July 31, 1943.
225. It should be noted that at this point there were no residents in Gatewood Gardens and that it was, in fact, located in Pigeon Township.
226. *Press*, September 7, 1943.
227. Ibid., September 10, 1943.
228. Ibid., September 14 and 15, 1943. The term "Federal Public Works" was presumably a reference to the Federal Works Agency, which used the Defense Housing and Community Facilities and Services Act of October 1940 (the "Lanham Act") to carry out a wide range of policies during the war, many of them related to children, education and housing.
229. Ibid., September 18, 1943.
230. Ibid., September 21, 1943; *Courier*, September 22, 1943.
231. *Press*, December 1, 1943; December 10, 1943.
232. Kellar and Kellar, *Evansville Shipyard*, 142.
233. The same schooling problem arose again with the new project of Diamond Villa; once again, Joe Graddy had to explain the situation. *Press*, October 5, 1944.
234. *Press*, April 6, 1944.
235. Ibid., April 4, 1944.
236. *Courier*, June 26, 1944.
237. Ibid., June 26, 1944.
238. *Press*, November 22, 1944.
239. Ibid., August 16, 1945.
240. Ibid., March 15, 1960.

## CHAPTER 6

241. *Courier*, November 10, 1945. This number was a product of an "unofficial compilation by the *Courier*."
242. Ibid., May 5, 1942.
243. *Press*, July 20, 1944.
244. Ibid., September 6, 1945.
245. *Courier*, August 25, 1944; *Press*, January 7, 1944.

246. *Press*, May 30, 1945.

247. Olmsted, *From Institute to University*, 130–31.

248. Ibid.

249. Hale, *Evansville College*, 1–2.

250. Hale, *Annual Report*, 1.

251. Olmsted, *From Institute to University*, 132–33; Klinger, *We Face the Future Unafraid*, 79.

252. Craven and Cate, *Army Air Forces in World War II*, 430.

253. Ibid., 427. Throughout the 1930s, the AAF as a percentage of the U.S. Army ranged from 9.7 percent to 11.9 percent. United States Army Air Forces (Office of Statistical Control, *Army Air Forces Statistical Digest*, 15).

254. Craven and Cate, *Army Air Forces*, 331.

255. Kennedy, *Freedom from Fear*, 229–30.

256. Mireles, *Aviation Accidents*, x. One man who spent at least some of his service investigating military air crashes was former Evansville College student First Lieutenant Earl Deig of the U.S. Marines. One accident that he investigated in California in 1943 was caused by material from a cleaning rag getting tangled in the aileron cables. Earl ended up fighting in the Battle of Saipan, where he earned a Purple Heart and ran into several old friends from Evansville (Deig, *A Story Not to be Forgotten*).

257. Pierce, "Earning their Wings."

258. Mireles, *Aviation Accidents*, xi.

259. United States Adjutant-General's Office, *Army Battle Casualties*, 100, 102.

260. *Press*, March 17 and 30, 1942; *Courier*, March 24, 1942.

261. *Courier*, December 8, 1943.

262. *Press*, January 4, 1946.

263. After the war was over, the Red Cross Canteen was moved to the campus of Evansville College, where it served as the Veterans Lounge; it played various roles on campus thereafter until finally being removed in 1965.

264. *Press*, July 1, 1943; *Courier*, June 24, 1944.

265. *Sunday C&P*, March 26 and June 25, 1944; *Press*, January 26, 1944; *Crescent*, April 5, 1944.

266. *Press*, August 25, 1944; *Sunday C&P*, August 26, 1945; American Air Museum in Britain. "Max K Thompson Jr."

267. *Press*, November 11, 1943; April 12, April 30, May 26 and October 27, 1945; *Courier*, December 4, 1943.

268. American Battle Monuments Commission, *American Memorials*, 4. See also Robin, "'A Foothold in Europe.'"

269. *Courier*, August 22, 1977.

270. Dreazen and Fields, "How We Bury the War Dead."

271. Steere, *Graves Registration Service*, 206.

272. *Courier*, April 26, 1946.

273. Sledge, *Soldier Dead*, 167.

274. "War Dead," *Life*, November 3, 1947, 77.

275. *Press*, October 10, 1947.

276. *Courier*, October 11, 1947. It is worth noting that the Funkhouser Post is named for two Evansville brothers, Paul and Albert, who were killed in the First World War.

277. *U.S. Department of Defense News Release No. 937-10.*

278. *Dayton Daily News*, October 16, 2010.

279. *Sunday C&P*, June 24, 1945.

280. Keegan, *Second World War*, 5.

281. Hale, *Annual Report.*

282. *Sunday C&P*, June 24, 1945.

283. *Courier*, January 19, 1951.

284. Ibid., September 23, 1946.

285. *Courier*, October 15, 2005. One of the crewmen who sailed LST 325 into Evansville was World War II veteran Bill Arras, who said, on the eve of their final arrival, "Evansville is where I wanted it. It's wonderful, absolutely wonderful."

# BIBLIOGRAPHY

American Air Museum in Britain. "Max K. Thompson Jr." http://www.americanairmuseum.com/person/157178 (accessed May 14, 2015).

American Battle Monuments Commission. *American Memorials and Overseas Military Cemeteries*. Washington, D.C.: American Battle Monuments Commission, 1985.

Ayer, Hugh. "Hoosier Labor in the Second World War." *Indiana Magazine of History* 59, no. 2 (June 1963): 95–120.

Babauta, Juan N. *In Remembrance and Honor of the Brave US Servicemen Who Made the Ultimate Sacrifice in the Marianas Campaign During World War II*. Washington, D.C.: Commonwealth of Northern Mariana Islands, Office of Resident Representative to the United States, 1997.

Bigham, Darrel E. *An Evansville Album: Perspectives on a River City, 1812–1988*. Bloomington: Indiana University Press, 1988.

———. "The Evansville Economy and the Second World War." *Traces of Indiana and Midwestern History* 3 (Fall 1991): 26–29.

———. *Evansville: The World War II Years*. Charleston, SC: Arcadia Publishing, 2005.

———. *We Ask Only a Fair Trial: A History of the Black Community of Evansville, Indiana*. Bloomington: Indiana University Press, 1987.

Blackburn, George M. "The Hoosier Arsenal." PhD diss., Indiana University, 1957.

Brandt, Allan M. *No Magic Bullet: A Social History of Venereal Disease in the United States Since 1880*. New York: Oxford University Press, 1985.

Burgoon, Janet S. *Memoranda to Eliot Ness, Federal Social Protection Division*. National Archives. Copy in Evansville Museum Archives.

Cavnes, Max. *The Hoosier Community at War*. Bloomington: Indiana University Press, 1961.

Churchill, Winston. *Memoirs of the Second World War: An Abridgement of the Six Volumes of the Second World War*. Boston: Houghton Mifflin, 1959.

Clark, Andrew. *A Cornfield Shipyard*. Mount Vernon, IN: Windmill, 1991.

Clark, Lloyd. *Anzio: Italy and the Battle for Rome—1944*. New York: Grove Press, 2006.

Coates, John Boyd, Ebbe Curtis Hoff, S.B. Hays and Phebe M. Hoff. *Communicable Diseases*. Washington, D.C.: Office of the Surgeon General, 1958.

Coates, John Boyd, Ebbe Curtis Hoff and Phebe Margaret Hoff. *Preventive Medicine in World War II. Vol. 5*. N.p., 1955.

Craven, Wesley Frank, and James Lea Cate. *The Army Air Forces in World War II. Vol. 6*. Chicago: University of Chicago Press, 1948.

Davies, Norman. *No Simple Victory: World War II in Europe, 1939–1945*. New York: Viking, 2007.

Deig, Jeffrey E. "A Story Not to Be Forgotten." Unpublished manuscript, 2008.

Ditmore, Melissa Hope. *Prostitution and Sex Work*. Santa Barbara, CA: Greenwood, 2011.

Doughty, Robert A. *World War II: Total Warfare Around the Globe*. Lexington, MA: D.C. Heath and Co., 1996.

Dreazen, Yochi, and Gary Fields. "How We Bury the War Dead." *Wall Street Journal*, May 29, 2010.

Employees' War Production Committee, Inc. Missouri Valley Bridge and Iron Company. *A Pictorial History of the Evansville Shipyard, January, 1942 to December, 1944*. N.p., n.d.

Fallows, James. "The Tragedy of the American Military." *Atlantic*, January/February 2015.

Federal Security Agency Office of Community War Services Region VI. *Report on Evansville*. 1943.

Feurer, Rosemary. *Radical Unionism in the Midwest, 1900–1950*. Urbana: University of Illinois Press, 2006.

Finney, Burnham. *Arsenal of Democracy; How Industry Builds Our Defense*. New York: Whittlesey House, McGraw-Hill Book Co., 1941.

Folly, Martin H. *The Palgrave Concise Historical Atlas of the Second World War*. New York: Palgrave-Macmillan, 2004.

Friedman, Bernard. *The Financial Role of Indiana in World War II*. Bloomington: Indiana University Press, 1966.

Fussell, Paul. *Wartime: Understanding and Behavior in the Second World War*. New York: Oxford University Press, 1989.

Gabin, Nancy Felice. "Women Defense Workers in World War II: Views of Gender Equality in Indiana." In *The Home-Front War: World War II and American Society*. Edited by Kenneth Paul O'Brien and Lynn H. Parsons. Westport, CT: Greenwood Press, 1995.

Glenday, Craig. *Guinness World Records 2015*. 2015.

Gourley, Harold E. *Shipyard Work Force: World's Champion LST Builders on the Beautiful Ohio, 1942–1945, Evansville, IN*. Evansville, IN: LST Work Force, 1996.

Hale, Lincoln B. *Annual Report of the President*. University of Evansville Archives, 1942.

————. *Evansville College Faces the War Years. An Address to the Student Body and Faculty on January 12, 1942*. University of Evansville Archives, 1942.

Harris, James R. "Rolling Bandages and Building Thunderbolts: A Woman's Memories of the Kentucky Home Front, 1941–45." *Register of the Kentucky Historical Society* 100, no. 2 (Spring 2002): 167–94.

Harrison, Gordon A. *Cross-Channel Attack*. Washington, D.C.: Office of the Chief of Military History, Department of the Army, 1951.

Hegarty, Marilyn E. "Patriot or Prostitute? Sexual Discourses, Print Media, and American Women during World War II." *Journal of Women's History* 10, no. 2 (Summer 1998): 112–36.

Hewitt, Nick. "The Role of the LST." TV Interview, PBS *Nova*. May 2014.

Hyde, Charles K. *Arsenal of Democracy: The American Automobile Industry in World War II*. Detroit, MI: Wayne State University Press, 2013.

Igleheart, Diane. Phone interview. Evansville, IN, May 20, 2015.

Johnsen, Frederick A. *Republic P-47 Thunderbolt*. North Branch, MN: Specialty Press, 1999.

Joint Army-Navy Release. *Army-Navy "Evansville" Award Termination Sees Award Granted to 5% of Eligible Plants*. N.p.: War Employment Bureau of Public Relations Press Branch, 1945.

Keegan, John. *The Second World War*. New York: Viking, 1990.

Kellar, James H., and Patricia C. Kellar. *The Evansville Shipyard: Outside Any Shipbuilding Zone*. Bloomington, IN: Round Hill Press, 1999.

Kennedy, David M. *Freedom from Fear. Part II, The American People in World War II*. New York: Oxford University Press, 1999.

Kersten, Andrew Edmund. *Labor's Home Front: The American Federation of Labor During World War II*. New York: New York University Press, 2006.

———. *Race, Jobs, and the War: The FEPC in the Midwest, 1941–46*. Urbana: University of Illinois Press, 2000.

Kitchen, Martin. *A World in Flames: A Short History of the Second World War in Europe and Asia, 1939–1945*. 1990.

Klein, Maury. *A Call to Arms: Mobilizing America for World War II*. New York: Bloomsbury Press, 2013.

Klinger, George. *We Face the Future Unafraid: A Narrative of the University of Evansville*. Evansville, IN: University of Evansville Press, n.d.

"Launching Program." *Invader* 1, no. 1 (October 1942): 6–7.

Leland, Anne. *American War and Military Operations Casualties: Lists and Statistics*. Washington, D.C.: Congressional Research Service, Library of Congress, 2010.

Lewin, Ronald. *Ultra Goes to War: The First Account of World War II's Greatest Secret Based on Official Documents*. London: Grafton, 1988.

Liberty Engineering Company. *Appraisal of Navy Department Property at Wabash and Ohio Streets, Evansville*. 1946. National Archives. Copy in the Evansville Museum Archives.

Linder, Marc. "Fatal Subtraction: Statistical MIA's on the Industrial Battlefield." *Journal of Legislation* 20, no. 2 (1994).

Lyons, Michael J. *World War II: A Short History*. Upper Saddle River, NJ: Pearson Prentice Hall, 2004.

Madison, James. *Indiana through Tradition and Change: A History of the Hoosier State and Its People, 1920–1945*. Indianapolis: Indiana Historical Society, 1982.

———. *The Indiana Way: A State History*. Bloomington: Indiana University Press, 1986.

———. *A Lynching in the Heartland: Race and Memory in America*. New York: Palgrave, 2003.

McCutchan, Kenneth, Thomas Lonnberg and William Bartelt. *Evansville at the Bend in the River: An Illustrated History*. Sun Valley: American Historical Press, 2004.

Mireles, Anthony J. *Fatal Army Air Forces Aviation Accidents in the United States, 1941–1945*. Jefferson, NC: McFarland, 2006.

Morgan, Harold B. *Home Front Heroes: Evansville and the Tri-State in WWII*. Evansville, IN: M.T. Publishing Co., 2007.

———. *Home Front Warriors: Building the P-47 Thunderbolt and the LST Warship in Evansville, Indiana During World War II*. Evansville, IN: Harold B. Morgan, 2011.

Morlock, James E. *The Evansville Story, A Cultural Interpretation*. Evansville, IN: Creative Press, 1956.

NavSource Naval History. "Self-propelled Barracks Ship APB-46 Dorchester." Photo Archive Main Index. http://www.navsource.org/archives/10/13/1346.htm (accessed April 30, 2015).

O'Brien, Kenneth Paul, and Lynn H. Parsons. *The Home-Front War: World War II and American Society*. Westport, CT: Greenwood Press, 1995.

O'Connor, Patrick, ed. *Built Strong. An Oral History Commemorating the 50th Anniversary of Industrial Contractors, Inc*. Evansville, IN: Skanska USA, 2015.

Office of Defense Health and Welfare Services, Region VI. *Report on Evansville War Production Area, Indiana*. 1942. National Archives. Copy in Evansville Museum Archives.

Ohly, John H., and Clayton D. Laurie. *Industrialists in Olive Drab: The Emergency Operation of Private Industries During World War II*. Washington, D.C.: Center of Military History, U.S. Army, 2000.

Olmsted, Ralph. *From Institute to University*. Evansville, IN: University of Evansville Press, 1973.

Panicello, Joseph Francis. *A Slow Moving Target: The LST of World War II*. N.p.: Authorhouse, 2002.

Patterson, Dan, and Paul Perkins. *Thunderbolt: Republic P-47*. Charlottesville, VA: Howell Press, 1999.

Pierce, Marlyn R. "Earning Their Wings: Accidents and Fatalities in the United States Army Air Force during Flight Training in World War Two." PhD diss., Kansas State University, 2013.

Reynolds, Ryan, ed. *LST 325: Workhorse of the Waves & Evansville's War Machine, 1942–45*. Evansville, IN: Evansville Courier and Press, 2005.

Robin, Ron. "'A Foothold in Europe': The Aesthetics and Politics of American War Cemeteries in Western Europe." *Journal of American Studies* 29, no. 1 (1995): 55–72.

Sanders, Gold V. "Push-Over Bridges Built Like Magic from Interlocking Parts." *Popular Science*, October 1944.

Scutts, Jerry. *Combat Legend Republic P-47 Thunderbolt*. Ramsbury, Wiltshire: Airlife Pub, 2003.

Sebag-Montefiore, Hugh. *Enigma: The Battle for the Code*. New York: Wiley, 2001.

Sharpe, Mike. *Aircraft of World War II*. Osceola, WI: MBI Pub. Co., 2000.

Sledge, Michael. *Soldier Dead: How We Recover, Identify, Bury, and Honor Our Military Fallen*. New York: Columbia University Press, 2005.

Steere, Edward. *The Graves Registration Service in World War II*. Washington, D.C.: Historical Section, Office of the Quartermaster General, 1951.

St. Louis, Ralph. "A Tale of Two Sisters." New Oxford Review, last modified November 1993. http://www.newoxfordreview.org/reviews.jsp?did=1193-stlouis.

Stoler, Mark A., and Melanie S. Gustafson. *Major Problems in the History of World War II: Documents and Essays*. Boston: Houghton Mifflin, 2003.

"The Story of the Evansville Shipyard." *Invader*, October 31, 1942.

Stout, Wesley Winans. *Bullets by the Billion*. Detroit, MI: Chrysler Corporation, 1946.

Sulzberger, C.L. *World War II*. New York: American Heritage, 1985.

Thomson, Harry C. *The Ordnance Department: Procurement and Supply*. Washington, D.C.: Office of the Chief of Military History, Department of the Army, 1960.

Tucker, Spencer. *The Second World War*. Houndmills, Basingstoke, Hampshire: Palgrave Macmillan, 2004.

Turner, Lynn W. "Indiana in World War II. A Progress Report." *Indiana Magazine of History* 52, no. 1 (1956): 1–20.

Turner, Lynn W., and Heber P. Walker. *Indiana at War; a Directory of Hoosier Civilians Who Held Positions of Responsibility in Official, Volunteer, and Cooperating War-time Organizations*. Bloomington: Indiana War History Commission, 1951.

United States Adjutant-General's Office. *Army Battle Casualties and Nonbattle Deaths in World War II. Final Report, 7 December 1941–31 December 1946*. Washington: Department of the Army, 1953.

United States Army Air Forces. Office of Statistical Control. *Army Air Forces Statistical Digest: World War II*. 1945.

United States Bureau of the Census. *Statistical Abstract of the United States, 1947*. Washington, D.C.: U.S. GPO, 1947.

*U.S. Department of Defense News Release No. 937-10*. October 14, 2010.

U.S. Department of Transportation, National Highway Traffic Safety Administration. *An Analysis of the Significant Decline in Motor Vehicle Traffic Fatalities in 2008*. Washington, D.C.: U.S. Department of Transportation, 2010. http://www-nrd.nhtsa.dot.gov/Pubs/811346.pdf.

U.S. Maritime Commission Regional Construction Office. *Re-Survey of Missouri Valley Bridge and Iron Company, Evansville, Indiana. April, 1944*. National Archives. Copy in Evansville Museum Archives.

Van Ells, Mark D. *To Hear Only Thunder Again: America's World War II Veterans Come Home*. Lanham, MD: Lexington Books, 2001.

"The War Dead." *Life*, November 3, 1947.

Weinberg, Gerhard L. *A World at Arms: A Global History of World War II*. Cambridge, UK: Cambridge University Press, 1994.

White, Samuel William. *Fragile Alliances: Labor and Politics in Evansville, Indiana, 1919–1955*. Westport, CT: Praeger Publishers, 2005.

Williams, Andrew. *The Battle of the Atlantic: Hitler's Gray Wolves of the Sea and the Allies' Desperate Struggle to Defeat Them*. New York: Basic Books, 2003.

Williams, Clendel. *Echoes of Freedom: Builders of LSTs, 1942–1945, United States Navy Shipyard, Evansville, Indiana*. Kearney, NE: Morris Publishing, 2011.

"World War Two and the LST Shipyard." *Picture This*. Directed by Jason Bumm and Brad Kimmel. Evansville, IN: WNIN PBS, February 5, 2015.

Zeiler, Thomas W. *Annihilation: A Global Military History of World War II*. New York: Oxford University Press, 2011.

# INDEX

Piper, Melvin 54
Prues, L.J. 86

## R

Rawlings, Dora Hess 73
Redgrave, DeWitt 39
Ritzert, Roman 41
Robinson, Jeanne 74
Rogers, William 89
Roosevelt, Franklin Delano 23, 27, 46, 102
Rose, Conrad 113
Ruthenburg, Louis 20, 25, 59

## S

Schnute, W.G. 91, 93
Schricker, Henry F 40
Servel 12, 14, 16, 20, 22, 23, 24, 25, 52, 59, 60, 70, 85, 103, 116, 119
Shane Manufacturing 52, 61
Shroeder, J. Henry 59
Smith, C. Nelson 24, 25, 26
Smith, Douglas 64
Smith, Lucy 64
Snyder, John W. 116
Spencer, John W. 83, 84
Steinback, William 100
Stein, Theo 85
Stimson, Henry 59
Strouse, Elise 73
Sunbeam 12, 14, 22, 23, 50, 57, 58, 59, 60, 64, 66, 73, 74, 103, 116, 119
Sweet, A.F. 96, 97

## T

Thirwell-Henderson-Marine 61
Thompson, Max, Jr. 102, 110
Truman, Harry S. 113

## V

Vanaman, A.W. 54
Vick, Talmadge 65

## W

Walton, John 89
Warren, Leo 91
Welborn, Mrs. James 92
Wilcox, George James 17, 100
Wilks, August 22
Wimsatt, George 108
Wolf, Harold W. 17, 113
Wright, Donald H. 110

# ABOUT THE AUTHOR

James Lachlan MacLeod was educated at the University of Edinburgh in Scotland. He taught history and British studies at Harlaxton College from 1994 to 1999 and since 1999 has been a member of the History Department at the University of Evansville. He conducts research and teaches courses in European history and the two world wars and lectures frequently on these topics. He has written a book on nineteenth-century British religion, *The Second Disruption* (2000), as well as many other scholarly publications. Dr. MacLeod is currently working on another book—on the longtime editorial cartoonist of the *Evansville Courier*, Karl Kae Knecht—which is being published by The History Press in 2016. He lives in Evansville with his family.